book is to be returned on or bef

the last date stamped below

RUNNING
RACING

Arcade Room, Jockey Club. Drawn by F. G. Kitton.

The Vodofone Derby Stakes 1997. Silver Patriarch (Pat Eddery) and Benny the Dip (Willie Ryan - the winner) fight out the finish.   Photo: Gerry Cranham

RUNNING RACING

THE JOCKEY CLUB YEARS
SINCE 1750

John Tyrrel

Foreword by Lord Hartington
final chapter by Michael Tanner

Quiller Press
London

For Becca

The Publishers would like to thank the following members of the Jockey Club for their generous assistance:
His Grace the Duke of Devonshire
Sheikh Hamdan bin Rashid al Maktoum
Lord Howard de Walden
Prince Khalid bin Abdullah
Lord Leverhulme
Paul Mellon
Sir Evelyn de Rothschild
Lord Vestey

The Publishers would also like to thank Michael Tanner for writing the final chapter 'Revolution' to bring the book up to date after the death of John Tyrrel.

(M) 636. 100 9 T
(m) 636-115 T

First published 1997 by Quiller Press Ltd
46 Lillie Road, London SW6 1TN

ISBN 01 899163 06 9

Designed by Jo Lee
Printed by Colorcraft Ltd. Hong Kong

Contents

"Stoker" Hartington.

Foreword *by the Marquess of Hartington*

Tragically John Tyrrel died before he had fully completed this book. However, with the assistance of Michael Tanner writing the last chapter, he has left racing an interesting and timely appraisal of the history of the Jockey Club. I should, perhaps, point out that the book was not commissioned by the Jockey Club and the authors were given free rein to select their own material and express their own views.

Like many British institutions, the Jockey Club came into existence to fulfil a very different role to that which latterly – since the first World War at least – it has taken on. The biggest change both to the Jockey Club and to racing in this country, occurred with the legislation of off course betting in 1961. That was the moment when the sport became an industry, although I must be careful as there are still many owners, and I suspect a few trainers and jockeys, who quite reasonably still regard racing as a sport and not as a business. Under the 1961 Act racing provided and continues to provide a major proportion of the raw material required by the betting industry to fill their betting shops.

Reading this book, it is impossible not to be reminded of the precarious way in which racing's finances have developed. It is remarkable that British racing is still a success and as popular as it is bearing in mind that it has by any reasonable standard been starved of funds for many years. British racing is still admired throughout the world although our prize money is poor in comparison. British racing is admired because of its traditions, its history and its straightness, and for this the Jockey Club must take a great deal of credit. Now that the club has returned to the role to which it is most suited, that of regulation, I am confident that it will continue to secure the admiration for British racing that it has achieved over the past 235 years.

I hope that the combination of the Jockey Club and the British Horseracing Board, separate but inter-dependent organisations, will make a formidable and successful partnership in the service of British racing.

Hartington

7th January 1997

The Byerley Turk, The Godolphin Arabian and the Darley Arabian. All racehorses in England, thanks to the Stud Book, can trace their origins back to those three which were brought to England in the late 17th and early 18th centuries at a time when producing horses for a rapidly expanding sport was becoming big business.

CHAPTER 1

Kings and Emperors

Since the dawn of civilisation, mankind has raced horses. Racing was an important event at the ancient Greek Olympiads, the Arabs have matched their steeds for centuries and a weekend in Rome was not complete without a sortie to the Circus Maximus in the days when the natives of yet unconquered Britain were matching shades of coloured earth and plant juice for woad whilst wondering why square cartwheels obstinately refused to rotate.

None the less, the horse played a great part in the lives of these primitives. When the Phoenicians, the prime traders of the world, dealt with the Britons for the tin and lead mined in Cornwall, they tipped off the Gauls and Belgians who arrived in Kent to find the British Standard to be a picture of a white horse. During the Belgic period which following during the first century BC. British art reached a magnificent peak, especially in metalwork.

The Britons could break and manage horses with an ability which has lasted to this very day, and the animals served them well in their battles against the Roman invaders in 55 BC and AD 43. In the course of the occupation, Roman garrisons sprang up and to amuse the troops, racing was organised. Of these early tracks, only Chester and York survive.

Following the departure of the Romans under Emperor Constantine III in 409, Britain fell into a rather dreary dark age of rule by Angles, Saxons and Jutes, only alleviated by the arrival of another conqueror, William, Duke of Normandy. Life under the Normans and Plantagenets may not have been all mead and wenches, but it was more lively than the gloom engendered by such monarchs as Canute the Dane, Alfred and Harold, to say nothing of the shadowy Arthur, who's chief claim to fame seems to be that he never existed.

Racing surfaced again during the reign of Henry II at Smithfield, then a horse market. The animals were tried in couples around the field, to demonstrate their physique and abilities to potential purchasers. This inevitably led to racing and organised meetings were held on public holidays.

Richard II in one of his rare light moments rode a winner at Smithfield, where the prize money was on a suitably royal scale, to judge from the following extract from the legend of Sir Bevis Hampton, describing the Whitsuntide Meeting:

> Which horses that best may run,
> Three myles the course was then,
> Who that might ride him shoulde
> Have forty pounds of redy gold…

Doubtless the grim-faced ill-sleeping Henry IV who succeeded Richard soon put a stop to that, to say nothing of later domestic upsets such as the Wars of the Roses, but by Tudor times the action had moved back to the old Roman course at Chester, where racing for a wooden ball gave way to a contest for a silver bell, value three shillings and fourpence, in 'the third year of the reign of Henry VIII', ie 1511.

A century later, Lady Dacre, wife of the Governor of Carlisle, donated a prize at the annual race meeting. Her gold bell, charmingly inscribed 'The Swiftes Horse this Bel to take for my Lade Dacre's sake' is the oldest racing trophy remaining open for competition, now known as the Carlisle Bell – albeit a replica. Happily, Lady Dacre's original bell has been preserved.

Lady Dacre presented her prize in 1619, sixteen years after James I of England and VI of Scotland came to the throne in succession to Elizabeth I. The Virgin Queen enjoyed her racing, taking in a day's sport at Salisbury when on a Progress to have a final tactical natter with Sir Francis Drake before the defeat of the Armada.

King James was not a natural sportsman and a poor rider, but his enthusiasm outweighed his incompetence. It says much for his courage in the field that he took in good part a nearly lethal ducking when thrown over his horse's head into an icy river 'Despite much water coming out of his mouth and body'. James restored hunting to its rightful place as a field sport, as opposed to the miserable slaughter of the 'battue' or enclosed parkland from which the quarry could not escape so favoured by the Elizabethans, and it is fair to say that he founded the Headquarters of Racing.

Not that James was so much of a racing man himself, but many of his courtiers were and when he became lost during a hare course near Fordham in Suffolk, he put up for the night at the Griffin Inn at an obscure market town called, in those days, New-Market. When the dawn finally broke on the morning of 28th February 1605 and the mists cleared from the heath, the King realised that he had stumbled across ideal sporting country.

He promptly purchased The Griffin and moved his court to New-Market, much to the annoyance of his officers of state who had to make the weary journey to East Anglia in order to conduct government business.

The Griffin soon became too cramped for the King and his retinue, so he commissioned the building of a palace. From there James hawked and hunt-ed while his friends and courtiers matched and raced horses. The first recorded match race at Newmarket was on 8th March 1622.

Sadly three years later, the King was dying of the ague. He had done much to ensure the future of the sport, encouraging racing in public in many parts of the country and donating prizes in the form of silver bells on the Chester and Carlisle pattern. These venues became known as 'bell courses'.

However, rules were almost non-existent, with a few exceptions: anyone riding in leather breeches, the denim jeans of the period, faced disqualification as he was clearly not a gentleman. There were some races starting at level weights, usually ten stone, as opposed to catch-weights, and foul riding was often punished with imprisonment, which makes the present Rule 153 comparable to a slap on the bottom with a wet feather.

Also, James's geography was decidedly flimsy. He declared Hexham to be 'The Heart of All England' and a steeplechase of that name is run on the Co. Durham course today. On the other hand, he did not neglect the breeding of the racehorse and British blood was continually reinforced by the import of good horses from Europe, including gifts of stallions and broodmares with foals from Italy and Scandinavia, the latter a present from his father-in-law, the King of Denmark.

The King also gave £154 to purchase the Markham Arabian, and James's Master of the Horse, George Villiers, Duke of Buckingham was also active in the continental markets. In his other capacity as Lord High Admiral, Buckingham used the ships of the Royal Navy to transport the animals to England, an arrangement which did not go down well with the captains of the vessels concerned; naturally enough, since they had joined the Navy to serve King and country and not to spend their time avoiding the smell of horse droppings rising to the appropriately named poop deck.

The new King, Charles I had enjoyed his own residence in Newmarket since 1617, where he entertained lavishly by the simple ploy of asking each guest to supply a dish for the feasts. The finest contribution recorded was generally considered to be that of Lord George Goring who presented for Charles's birthday 'Foure huge brawny pigs, piping hot, bitted and harised with ropes and sarsiges, all tyde in a monstrous black pudding.' Charles survived this and similar assaults on his digestive tract with aplomb, but unhappily he did not avoid the headsman's axe on the scaffold in Whitehall.

He had looked upon Newmarket as a second home and during his reign the first grandstand was built on the Heath, the spring and autumn meetings were established in 1627 and he continued to conduct state business from the old palace. The famous Van Dyke and Rubens portraits of the King were painted there and Dr William Harvey made his discovery of the circulation of the blood while acting as Court Physician.

Oliver Cromwell now ruled Britain, and one of his first Acts punished adultery with death, but who would want to sleep with him anyway? This genial guardian of public morality prohibited racing in 1654, but in reality it was not allowed from the moment he seized power by force of arms in 1649. It is said that Cromwell had no puritanical aversion to racing, maintaining his own coach teams and a stud, the ban on race meetings stemming from the fear that such events might encourage crowds sympathetic to the royal cause.

If so the former brewer, happy enough to make money from the indulgences of his fellow countrymen whilst condemning them, and now Lord Protector, self-styled, was for once thwarted; races were staged at several places notably Epsom and the Isle of Man, where the award of a Derby Cup has caused much speculation that this was the original or at least the forerunner of the premier classic.

It was nothing of the sort. The Derby Stakes was first run in 1780 at Epsom and has no connection with earlier events or trophies, except that they bear the same family name.

The continuation of Cromwell's studs was probably no more than an example of socialist hypocrisy, with the rich 'man of the people' protecting his own commercial interests, a trait not unknown in Fabian politics today.

Having been restored to his rightful inheritance in 1660, with Cromwell mouldering in his grave, warts and all, King Charles II lost no time in reviving racing. However, he did not visit Newmarket for some years after his accession, probably because Cromwell's troops had left the palace in the poor condition customary to soldiers living in other people's property. There are churches in East Anglia which bear witness; the Roundheads thought nothing of stabling their horses in the nave or even the sanctuary.

The palace refurbished, Charles returned to HQ and took part in every activity, riding in matches, and founding the system of Royal Plates which an early form of patronage, or regal sponsorship. His most enduring innovation was the Newmarket Town Plate, still competed for annually and until 1971 the only surviving race open to lady riders under the sanction of the Jockey Club.

Neither the Club or anything like it existed in 1665, and it was to be nearly a century before 'Newmarket Rules', later known as Jockey Club Rules, gradually came into force. Even so, some code of conduct was required. It was at this time that betting, hitherto a matter of honour between gentlemen, came into the public domain although as yet without the dubious benefit of the bookmaking fraternity, which was not to be in evidence until about 1790.

Accordingly, the conditions of the Town Plate stated:

If any difference shall be about the riding for the Plate, it shall be referred to the noblemen and gentlemen which are then present and being contributors to the said Plate; but more especially the judges, the judge being chosen every time the Plate or prize is run for, by the majority of the contributors that are then present.

In the absence of any governing body, the King took it upon himself to

The last race run before Charles II. It was held at Windsor in 1684. Charles II was often seen on his hack named Old Rowley watching training gallops – hence the name Rowley Mile. King Charles rode in races, winning the Plate at Newmarket where the races would last two weeks and when those watching would often join in with his retinue for the last furlong or two.

adjudicate in disputes, his authority being absolute. He won the Town Plate on 14th October 1671 and also rode a winner at the Spring Meeting in 1675. Since then no reigning sovereign has ridden the winner of a recognised contest.

As with Charles's father and grandfather, affairs of state tended to be resolved at Newmarket, and then only 'in his bedroom, the privy or on waking from his post-prandial nap. There was little other time to spare from the pleasures of the bed, the table and the field'; or so said Thomas Conway, one of his chief ministers.

The King also frequented the Newmarket brothels, supposedly incognito. On one occasion, his pockets having been emptied in the usual way when engaged with a lady of the night, the embarrassed monarch could offer only a jewelled ring in payment. The madame immediately knocked up a local jeweller for valuation. 'Who gave you this?' said the night-shirted tradesman, magnifying glass in eye. 'Why, a black looking ugly rake' replied the madame. 'That,' said the jeweller who had recognised the ring, 'is the King of England.'

In 1683, fire swept the town, and Charles and his brother the Duke of York later James II fled the conflagration which was started by a stable lad smoking in Lord Sunderland's stables. Inadvertently, this saved their lives. At Hoddesdon in Hertfordshire, Rye House lay at a conveniently narrow point on the Newmarket Road. The Duke of Monmouth, Charles's illegitimate son by Lucy Walker, had planned an assassination to secure the throne for himself. The royal gentlemen's early departure foiled the plot.

Even so, time was running out for Charles. The following year he made his last visit to Newmarket, ladies conspicuous by their absence. He was now fifty-three, an old man by the standards of the time. His unhappy Queen, the Portuguese Catherine of Braganza, was unsurprisingly absent from the King's deathbed in 1685, but remembered by the Turf for the draft of Arab horses which were part of her dowry and swiftly absorbed in the restocking of the Royal studs after the neglect of Cromwell's Commonwealth.

James II had little effect on the Turf but he had greater concerns, principally the Catholic Church and the unsuccessful rebellion led by his aforementioned illegitimate nephew, the Duke of Monmouth. It is recorded that he attended Winchester races and Judge Jefferies, warming up for the Bloody Assizes, dispensed his own brand of brutal 'justice' to the unfortunate followers of Monmouth in Winchester's courts. During James's reign professional work riders were permitted to take part in minor races, the classier events remaining the preserve of gentlemen riders.

The condominion of William III and Mary initially showed little interest in racing, having to preside over the revolution of 1688 which eventually established the Protestant religion as the predominant national faith, while returning much of the administration of the country to the squirearchy and away from central government.

Following the death of Mary in 1694, William III decided to improve the palace at Newmarket, founded the Royal Stud at Hampton Court and took up gambling on a formidable scale. He staked up to two thousand guineas a time on matches featuring his horses which rejoiced in such names as Turk and Stiff Dick.

Newmarket dominated by the horse in the early eighteenth century. A line engraving by James Seymour shows the Watering Place with a string of horses owned by the Duke of Devonshire.

However, Newmarket which was the fountainhead of Turf affairs and the leading racecourse in the country, slid into something of a backwater, and the sport itself naturally followed. The administrative vacuum left by the death of Charles II had been filled by Tregonwell Frampton. Born in 1641, he lived for eighty-six years and served William and Mary, Queen Anne and Kings George I and II. As Keeper of the Running Horses he was effectively the royal trainer. It is not recorded, but Frampton might have trained for Charles II, as he would have been forty-four at the time of the monarch's death.

Frampton was a member of a sporting family from Moreton in Dorset. Not surprisingly, he was a devotee of cock-fighting and hare coursing, gambled heavily in four-figure sums and was not entirely scrupulous in his racing activities.

The most notorious case led to a change in the laws of England. Frampton struck a match with a Yorkshire baronet, Sir William Strickland, to run Strickland's horse Old Merlin against a favourite unnamed animal of Frampton's. Old Merlin was sent to Newmarket under the care of his jockey Heseltine and on their arrival Frampton suggested a trial at level weights. Heseltine declined, but on reporting back to his employer, was told to accept but to add seven pounds to Old Merlin's weight.

Tregonwell Frampton was kept on by Queen Anne as keeper of horses at Newmarket. Cock fighting was his other interest. Later William III made him Keeper of the Running Horses, a job compared to a modern racing manager, for which he got £1000 per year.

Old Merlin won the trial by a length, but Frampton was happy enough as he had also given his runner an extra seven pounds. Thinking he had about six lengths in hand, he betted accordingly. Unhappily, so did Frampton's many Newmarket followers. A great number were ruined and 'The Father of the Turf' himself received no mean 'staggerer' in the jargon of the time when Old Merlin duly won the match by a length, exactly reproducing the form of the trial.

As a result of the heavy losses sustained by the public 'The Legislature, in order to put a stop to such ruinous proceedings, enacted a law to prevent the recovery of any sum exceeding ten pounds betted on a horse race'. This was the forerunner of the original Gaming Act which prevents the recovery of any wager by law and is still in force.

Queen Anne had her problems, not the least being her gluttonous and overweight but virile husband, Prince George of Denmark. The Queen endured eighteen pregnancies and gave birth to six children, none of whom survived infancy, with one stillborn. Not surprisingly, she did not enjoy good health and was generally considered to be dull and uncharitable. However, she was a niece of Charles II and inherited his love of racing. She was also fortunate both militarily and politically and when the War of the Spanish Succession was effectively ended by the Duke of Marlborough's victories at Blenheim and Ramillies, peace came to Europe swiftly followed by the Act of Union with Scotland.

The ensuing period was a renaissance of art, science and literature accompanied by a revival in the fortunes of commerce and agriculture. The people were happy to relax and enjoy the sporting pleasures, including racing. The Queen patronised Newmaket and York, but will always be remembered for the foundation of Royal Ascot, the finest race meeting in the world in 1711.

Queen Anne did not live much longer to enjoy her amusement. She had sponsored a 100 guinea Gold Cup event at York in 1711, but an attempt to win the cash back was foiled when her grey gelding Pepper could only finish third after two heats, beaten by Farmer and Sturdy Lump. They knew how to name horses in those days.

Anne gained some compensation when Star won a £14 plate at York on Friday, 30th July 1714 but by now the monarch was close to death. On Monday, 2nd August, the news of her demise reached York and following the proclamation of George I as the next King, the nobility and the gentry left the Knavesmire and returned to London.

If Queen Anne had been a good friend to racing, her successor was not and the same can be said of George II, although both had horses in training with Tregonwell Frampton who doubtless arranged the running of the animals to his own pecuniary advantage.

Queen Anne, a great supporter of racing and founder of Royal Ascot and York.

During this period, three events formed the future of the sport. The first was the introduction of the *Calendar* in 1727 by John Cheney of Arundel. The publication was called 'An Historical List of All the Horse-Matches run, and All Plates and Prizes run for in England and Wales (of a value of ten pounds and upwards)' and included a record of the principal cock-fights.

The volume was a good buy at five shillings, even if the cost would be over £90 today, which is still not unreasonable – *Timeform Annual* is now £65 or so. Mr Cheney was at pains to point out that 'not only would it be an agreeable amusement for Gentlemen to divert themselves, in the midst of winter, with the prospect, as it were, of the sport next year but they would also discover what figure each particular horse had made at the Places of his Running the Season before; what alterations, different weights and different courses and different seasons of the year had caused in any of them.

'From hence' (he continued) ''twill be always discoverable what old Horses are dropping and how they decline and go off; what young Horses are every year coming up; and by what steps they advance and improve. Which render

Gentlemen capable of reducing their calculations nearer to perfection, and consequently of matching or betting with greater advantage.'

As Roger Mortimer pointed out, Mr Cheney's work seems more in line with *Raceform* or *Timeform* that the staid and severely factual *Calendar* of today, although it is fair to say than the official organ of the Jockey Club is not intended to provide entertainment, only occasionally and unwittingly doing so.

The second event came about because of the greater publicity which racing attracted following the publication of the *Calendar*. News of the sport, still largely based at Newmarket, started to appear in the daily papers, and interest rapidly spread throughout the country: so much so that in 1740 Parliament passed an Act placing restrictions on racing which Sir Robert Walpole and his friends at Westminster had rather arbitarily decided was becoming too popular for the common good.

No doubt they acted with the best of intentions, and certainly there was a good deal of malpractice of the 'gaff' tracks. The Act fixed the minimum value a plate at £50, also stipulating the weights to be carried.

Five-year-olds were burdened with ten stone, six-year-olds eleven, seven-year-olds and upwards carried twelve. The owner of any runner failing to draw the correct weight was fined £200 and forfeited the horse.

An example of matches – the original races. This is the famous Hambletonian – Diamond match on the 4 mile 2 furlong Beacon Course at Newmarket for the princely sum of 3000 guineas, 1799. Side betting was estimated between 200,000 and 300,000 guineas.

Matches were allowed at Newmarket and Black Hambledon near Thirsk only. Hambledon was then the principal racecourse in the north which ironically was badly hit by the Act, the number of races run being reduced from 36 to 6 in a single year. Hambledon was forced to give way and the fixtures were transferred to York in 1779.

For the matches, a minimum stake of £50 was again specified. Finally, Parliament relied on the common informer for evidence, the spy reporting malpractice to the authorities receiving half the fine and the other half being allocated for the benefit of the poor of the parish concerned.

Although this breathtaking piece of legislative interference failed entirely and deservedly to prevent the spread of racing – ten years later there were meetings in almost every county in the country – it was clear that the sport required a regulatory body or otherwise Parliament would take control anyway. A similar dilemma was to arise two hundred and fifty years later when the Parliamentary threat of a statutory British Racing Authority prompted the formation by the Jockey Club of the British Horseracing Board.

The Oaks, the 12th Earl of Derby's house, which gave the name to the race.

The third significant event of the early Georgian period was as a consequence of a similar threat, the birth of the Jockey Club. Then as now there were sportsmen prepared to take up the challenge. They were not known as the Jockey Club of course, but were a disparate group of gentlemen with a common interest in the Turf lounging elegantly in the coffee houses of St James's and mostly at the Star and Garter in Pall Mall. This last-mentioned establishment was noted for its good but expensive cuisine and choice selection of wines.

It is interesting to note how frequently gastronomy finds a niche in the history of racing's institutions. Without the enterprise of William Lynn, known as the 'finest fish-cook in Europe' and proprietor of the Waterloo, a well-cellared hotel in Liverpool, there would have been no Grand National and no Waterloo Cup. If the famous dinner party to celebrate Bridget's victory in the inaugural Oaks at the eponymous country house had not taken place there would have been no Derby, and if Lord Rockingham had not held a similar session at his seat near Doncaster ostensibly to discuss nominations for the 1778 of the yet unnamed race, the St Leger would be the Rockingham.

But all this was in the future as the gentlemen of the Star and Garter prepared to issue their first edict.

CHAPTER 2

Emergence and Establishment

When John Cheney died in 1751, his Calendar was succeeded by the Sporting Kalendar, published by John Pond, an auctioneer with businesses in Covent Garden and Newmarket. In 1758, his daughter apparently caught the eye of that well-known country sports enthusiast Dr Samuel Johnson, who noted her 'equestrian prowess' in *The Idler*, a magazine of the period. The lady had ridden a horse for a thousand miles in a thousand hours to win a 200 guineas bet. The good doctor did not approve of the venal nature of the contest, but clearly admired Miss Pond.

In 1752, the *Kalendar* carried an announcement that: 'There will be run for, at Newmarket, on Wednesday, April 1st, 1752, a Contribution Free Plate, by horses the property of the noblemen and gentlemen belonging to the Jockey Club at the Star and Garter in Pall Mall.'

Perhaps one of the gentlemen decided that All Fools' Day might be both unlucky and inappropriate to the event, or perhaps there were other distractions. After all, the Star and Garter was the scene of an unfortunate quarrel between Lord Byron and Mr Chaworth, resulting in the death of the latter, where Lord Barrymore offered to eat a live cat for a bet, and where the Laws of Cricket were revised in 1774 – so there was always plenty of activity.

For whatever reason, the race did not take place until the Newmarket May Meeting in 1753, when two 'Jockey Club Plates' were run, both restricted to horses owned by members of the Club. The first race, on May 16th, was won by Lord Gower's bay colt, and the second event, on the following day, by Captain Vernon's Crabb.

Although there is no precise foundation date, it seems that by now the Jockey Club, like many excellent British institutions and all Tory Prime Ministers prior to Sir Edward Heath, had 'emerged'. Their meeting places were not confined to the Star and Garter; the Thatched House in St James's Street was a popular watering hole as was the Clarendon in Bond Street. The ubiquitous Richard Tattersall, of whom more later, provided a room and a cook at his horse mart situated on the Corner, Hyde Park and Tattersall later obliged with the same facilities when his business moved to Knightsbridge.

The name 'Jockey Club' has puzzled more than one observer over the years, since it is not a social club in the sense of Dr Johnson's 'Club' except when race meetings are in progress at Newmarket, and it is not an association of professional riders; indeed, no person who holds a professional licence of any sort under Rules can be admitted to membership until they have retired.

In the eighteenth century, it was customary to call members of the professions and trades by the description of their occupation, hence for instance Mr Justice Hangem for a judge, or Mr Sawyer Knothole for a tree feller or woodcutter. Any person who was in the management of or dealing with horses was known as Mr Jockie in the contemporary spelling, later becoming Mr Jockey Hookup or whatever.

It has also been suggested that members sported a special Club attire in the form of a brown coat, cut away and adorned with lettered gilt buttons, and it is known that as late as the 1850s some Stewards of the Club favoured such garments. Surtees writes in *Handley Cross* of Mr Strider attending the hunt dinner in 'a brown Newmarket cut-away with lettered buttons'.

However, bearing in mind that male attire between 1750 and 1850 was colourful enough, encompassing as it did the sartorially brilliant Regency period,

Rowlandson's Jockey Club shows up no individual members but gives an impression of the room in the late 18th century. As one industrialist commented, "To become a member of the Jockey Club you have to be a relative of God – and a close one at that." Indeed amongst the members at this time there was a prince, two royal dukes and nine other dukes – not to mention a marquess, earls, viscounts, barons etc.

it is doubtful if the brown coat was universally worn, useful though it might have been to identify members before the first official list was published in 1835.

One of the advantages of 'emergence' without any written constitution or manifesto is flexibility of action. As Robert Black points out in his excellent *The Jockey Club and its Founders* published in 1891, a manifesto was the undoing of the French version, the Société d'Encouragement, whose restrictive practices did much to dissipate the standard of the native breed.

Indeed, the Club did not set out to be legislators or reformers but simply to lay down a set of rules to protect racing from the undesirable members of society always attracted to games played for high stakes, and in so doing the Club unintentionally protected the genuine punter. The other aims and objects, as with any gentlemen's club, would have been good fellowship, good sport, decent port and an easy-going life on the Turf.

Eventually the Club's formal London headquarters were established at the offices of its agents, Messrs Weatherby in Old Bond Street. Metropolitan base and administrative secretariat secured, the Club sought a premises in which to meet at Newmarket. In 1752 they leased a plot of land and built the inevitable Coffee Room; and the Coffee Room in the present Club building in the High Street stands on the same site, beautifully restored and maintained. A fanciful imagination can picture the members seated in the alcoves specially designed to ensure privacy, sipping coffee and other restoratives as they made their matches and struck their wagers, later hacking or driving up to the Heath for a day's sport in the clear air of East Anglia.

But who were they? Certainly one member was Mr Jockie Vernon, otherwise Captain Richard Vernon and sometimes known as 'The Oracle of Newmarket'. He not only won the second of the inaugural Jockey Club Plates with Crabb, but also the first Jockey Club Challenge Cup with Marquis in 1768. Perhaps more importantly he took over the lease of the Coffee Room and the other members of the Club became his tenants.

The coffee room at the present Jockey Club premises in Newmarket.

Vernon's other claim to fame was his membership of the 'Bloomsbury Gang', a political group under the patronage of the Duke of Bedford who secured Vernon seats in Parliament representing Tavistock, Bedford and Oakhampton.

For this service, Vernon Place, Bloomsbury Square, is named after him. He married the Dowager Countess of Upper Ossory in 1759 and died in 1800 aged 85, but not before he had devised a sounding board mounted over the pulpit in his parish church at Newmarket which was designed to come down over the parson's head if Vernon thought the sermon was going on for too long.

RACING CALENDAR:

CONTAINING

An ACCOUNT of the

PLATES, MATCHES,

AND

SWEEPSTAKES,

Run for in GREAT-BRITAIN and IRELAND, &c. in the Year 1777.

TOGETHER WITH

An ABSTRACT of all the MATCHES, SWEEPSTAKES, &c. now made, to be Run at NEWMARKET, from the CRAVEN MEETING 1778, to the Year 1783.

AND OF

Several MATCHES, &c. made for YORK, BATH, and many other Places:

By JAMES WEATHERBY,

Keeper of the MATCH-BOOK at NEWMARKET.

VOLUME the FIFTH.

LONDON:

Printed by H. REYNELL, near Air Street, Piccadilly.

MDCCLXXVII.

The Racing Calendar still published by Weatherbys for the official data of forthcoming races.

Robert Black reckoned that he could record about one hundred or so members of the Club in the early days. In the absence of an official list, he relied upon signatures on documents, races confined to members and the somewhat dubious veracity of Charles Pigott, commonly known as 'Louse'. Pigott was the author of *The Jockey Club*, the first history. It is essentially a scurrilous account of the members and their less attractive habits. Not surprisingly, Pigott was asked to withdraw from the Jockey Club.

For the Club history and other libels published in Pigott's *Political Dictionary* which served politicians as he had served the Club members, his printer was imprisoned in 1763. Louse himself was incarcerated in Sumpter Prison for uttering seditious language. Falling into debt, he died in jail in 1794.

However he was a fine amateur rider, winning many races in his colours of 'yellow, shot with red' which he reckoned was the colour of his eyes and reflected his lurid sense of humour. A fearless gambler, he lost a fortune on the Turf.

Hardly a reliable source, his list of members published in *The Jockey Club* is open to question. Even so the nickname 'Louse' is not intended to be derogatory. Pigott earned the appellation at Eton where he showed a remarkable skill at French, which enabled him to translate 'pou' into the equivalent English.

Black's list of members spanned the years 1755 to 1773 which, as he remarks, is a convenient date as it was in that year that the long connection between the Club and Weatherbys' *Calendar* began. The list names eleven Dukes, including two Royal Dukes, twenty-nine Lords of varying rank (not all are peers), seventeen Sirs, i.e. Baronets and Knights and fifty-eight Messrs or Misters, ignoring military ranks and the title Honorable. Of these, two cannot be verified including Dr Johnson's diarist Boswell and four are Pigott's suggestions, so it would seem that the Club had a membership of 109 which could more or less be confirmed, compared to a total of around 136 today. Within the modern total are twelve Honorary members and ten former Members of the old National Hunt Committee which was amalgamated with the Jockey Club in 1968.

Allowing for the absence of honorary membership and steeplechasing during the first twenty years of the Club's existence, the figure is comparable. In what the modern media jargon would call a 'rank profile', excluding

Honorary Members and using Black's categories, Dukes have slumped to only two. There are just under a third fewer Lords with a similar decrease in Sirs. As one would expect in these democratic times, the Messrs ranks have swelled and there is a new category unthinkable in Louse Pigott's day: ladies. The distaff side now make up just over eight percent of the Club's membership, which in 1956 was only forty-nine. There is also one judge, the Hon. Mr Justice Connell.

Although Pigott unquestionably went too far even by the standards of his time in his attacks on fellow members, there can be little doubt that many were of flimsy moral virtue and disreputable in their way of life. This behaviour was not unusual for the upper classes, when men of wealth and rank indulged in foolish pastimes while two million pounds a year was being spent out of public funds for the relief of the poor. By contrast all other services met by local rates cost less than £200,000 per annum.

Horace Walpole probably summed up the general standard of behaviour amongst aristocrats when he remarked, 'A quarter of our peeresses will soon have been the wives of half our living peers.'

Naturally, this corruption came to influence public life, even if with hindsight it may have been over-stated, doubtless due to over-reporting. However, it is fortunate that the Jockey Club came into existence when it did, and we can take consolation in that the 'rakes' naturally enough took little part in the administration of the Turf. Since these 'fun-loving' gentlemen have tended to loom large in many racing annals and their antics well chronicled elsewhere, there seems little point in repetition. The exploits of such as the Lords Barrymore, known to their friends as 'Cripplegate', 'Newgate' and 'Hellgate', the Duke of Grafton, 'Old Q', the 'Star of Piccadilly', the first Earl of Grosvenor, the third Earl of Orford, Lord Foley and even Mr Charles James Fox were fascinating in their way, but they had only a passing acquaintance with the Jockey Club save for their membership.

The active members of the Club in the early years were headed by William, Duke of Cumberland, known to every schoolboy as the 'Butcher of Culloden'. He was the second son of George II and the first Royal member of the Club. As Ranger of Windsor Great Park he effectively controlled Ascot races and it was at Royal Lodge where he bred Eclipse, although unhappily he did not live to see the champion on a racecourse.

The Duke's foundation mares were Cypron, the dam of Herod, the Spiletta, the dam of Eclipse, thus providing two of the greatest stallions in the history of equine genealogy. With Dumplin in 1764 he became the earliest recorded winner of the Challenge Whip, confined to horses owned by members and still competed for today. The Whip has place of honour over the fireplace in the Coffee Room at Newmarket.

The third Duke of Ancaster, Master of the Horse to George III, was tireless in his efforts to improve the British thoroughbred, giving his stallions such generic names an Ancaster Starling, Ancaster Egyptian and the Ancaster Bay

Arabian, which ran in a race confined to Arab horses at Newmarket in 1771.

The Duke of Bridgwater, the great canal builder, was one of the signatories to the first public document issued by the Club in 1758. He was busy in Club affairs generally and on the racecourse, but had greater success as a breeder with his Cullen Arabian mare, dam of such equine luminaries of the time as Stripling, Grasshopper, Glancer and Spectre. An immensely rich man, as he drew a royalty for every barge which passed through his canals, Bridgwater paid £110,000 a year in income tax, a sum equivalent to over forty-one million in modern terms.

Naturally enough the Cavendish family were prominent in early times and continue to be so now. It was a Cavendish 'but then a Duke of Newcastle', as Black puts it, who taught Charles II to ride and wrote a celebrated treatise entitled 'Methode et Invention Nouvelle de Dresser les Chevaux'.

The family were created Dukes of Devonshire in 1694. The second Duke owned Flying Childers and shoals of winners with names such as Plasto and Basto, to say nothing of the 'Devonshire Arabians' imported or purchased by the family.

Both the fourth and fifth holders of the title were keenly involved in the Club. The fourth Duke was more successful on the racecourse when not serving briefly as Prime Minister, but the fifth incumbent had the reputation of being a scholar rather than a 'jockey', and it seems that several of his horses ran in the name of his wife, Georgiana, whos beauty inspired an ode by Coleridge. Robert Black hints that she may have been a member of the Club, but there is no proof and it is unlikely.

Despite his way of life, the Duke of Grafton has to command respect as a patron of the Turf, and was a successful owner and breeder, winning three Derbys and two runnings of the Oaks. He entertained members of the Club at his Norfolk seat, Euston, on a lavish scale, but it is doubtful if he had any more influence on the administrative affairs of racing than he had on the affairs of the nation when he was Prime Minister between 1768 and 1770.

Others who contributed to the Club in a practical way included the Duke of Hamilton, a fine amateur rider, and Lord Craven, after whom the Craven Stakes is named. Initially competed for in 1771 it was the first public race (ie not a match) in which two-year-olds were allowed to compete, whether against each other or against their seniors at what was to become known as the Craven Meeting at Newmarket.

The Earl of Upper Ossory, Sir John Kaye and Mr Henry Compton were all distinguished members, but none more so than Sir Charles Bunbury Bt. His influence on the Turf continues into modern times.

CHAPTER 3

The Bunburyists

S ir Charles Bunbury became the Steward of the Jockey Club at the age of twenty-eight in 1768 and the Club had been in existence for approximately sixteen years.

A system of election had been established. Candidates had to be proposed by two members and they were elected by ballot. A quorum of at least nine was required and two black balls in the ballot box would exclude the candidate.

This arrangement was rather upset when a certain Mr Brereton, described by Bunbury's wife the former Lady Sarah Lennox as 'a sad vulgar', accused none other than the great huntsman Hugo Meynell, together with 'Jockey' Vernon, of cheating at cards. A meeting to expel Brereton from the Club discovered that he was not a member and was merely paying a subscription for the use of the Coffee Room, ironically a ploy of Vernon's to increase profits. 'Jockey' should have been more select in his choice of company and it was hastily arranged that a ballot amongst the members would in future decide admissions to the Room.

Diomed, winner of the first Derby of 1780.

Sir Charles Bunbury, a Steward of the Jockey Club at 28, became known as the Perpetual President of the Club and the first 'Dictator of the Turf'. He was apparently a kind man though he sold off Diomed who had won the Derby for him, at the venerable age of 22, for a mere fifty guineas.

Various other reforms had been enacted. In 1756 heats for Jockey Club Plates had been abolished in the interests of more competitive racing and a system of weighing in after a race was introduced in 1758, two pounds over the allotted weight being allowed. Any excess attracted disqualification from riding at Newmarket, unless the overweight had been declared before the race.

Colours became mandatory in 1762 'for the greater convenience of distinguishing the horses in running and also for the prevention of disputes arising from not knowing the colours worn by each rider…'.

The colours agreed were as follows:

Duke of Cumberland	Purple
Duke of Grafton	Sky Blue
Duke of Kingston	Crimson
Duke of Ancaster	Buff
Duke of Bridgwater	Garter Blue
Marquis of Rockingham	Green
Earl of Waldegrave	Deep Red
Earl of Orford	Purple and White
Earl of March and Mr Vernon	White
Earl of Northumberland	Deep Yellow
Earl of Gower	Blue with Cap of ditto
Viscount Bolingbroke	Black
Sir J. Moore	Darkest Green
Mr Granville	Brown, trimmed Yellow
Mr Shafton	Pink
Lord Grosvenor	Orange
Sir J. Lowther	------

As Sir J. Lowther clearly could not make up his mind, it is hard to know why he figures on the list. Most of the colours derived from the livery worn by coachmen and only one cap is mentioned, as most livery included a simple black velvet cap, as worn in the hunting field today and also by Her Majesty's coachmen and outriders for the Royal Procession at Ascot.

Although there is no evidence that the Club as such had any direct involvement in the matter, the existence of a ruling body and a slowly emerging set of rules clearly influenced the first public 'warning-off' notice, published in the *Calendar* in 1770.

The Jockey Club's book of racing colours.

Chester Races

In order to save Mr Quick, Mr Castle or any of the Ascott confederacy the trouble and expense of training, they are desired to take notice that none of their horses will be allowed to run for any of the above Plates, neither will they be suffered to run for any of the Plates at Conway, Nantwich or Holywell; nor will Thomas Dunn be permitted to ride.

The Ascott confederacy were presumably a group of southern turfistes of a slightly 'warm' disposition who had landed a series of coups in the north-west to the discomfiture of the locals who were used to having such illegal benefits to themselves.

Reading between the lines, it was probably a case of the pot calling the kettle black, but the 'get your tractors off our lawn' attitude of the Chester worthies nonetheless gave impetus to the Jockey Club's burgeoning authority and reflected a similar system already in effect on Newmarket Heath designed to suppress the undesirable activities of 'touts' or work watchers. The Heath belonged largely to Jockey Club members even at this early stage, and therefore was private property. It followed that the training grooms were entitled to exercise and try their charges without uninvited onlookers. As a consequence, touts and other trespassers were warned off the Heath if caught.

Legally nothing has changed today, but it is amusing if not easy to envisage the press corps, TV crews and other hangers-on being warned off the Heath as, for instance, Henry Cecil prepares his classic candidates. Even so, there are some residents of the premier racing town who might wish this was the case, if only because it is impossible to assess the effect on the animals of all the media attention emanating from those not always versed in the ways of the thoroughbred.

More importantly, in 1771 the Club decided that 'all disputes relative to racing at Newmarket should be for the future decided by three Stewards, and by two Referees to be chosen by the parties concerned. Since Newmarket effectively embodied the sport at the time, the three Stewards were almost certainly acting for the Jockey Club as well, headed by Sir Charles Bunbury; this followed the order of 1770, published in the *Calendar* and reading as follows:

> It was resolved that the Members should meet annually at dinner on the day following the King's birthday, that three Members should be appointed as Stewards, to commence their office on 4th June annually; one new Steward to be appointed every year on 3rd June by the Steward who quits on that day, subject to the approbation of the Members of the Jockey Club then present; ever afterwards the Senior Steward is to quit the post on 3rd June annually.

The King at the time was George III, whose birthday was on 24th May, thus allowing ten days before the appointments had to be taken up. The 4th of June is Founders' Day at Eton, and this may have had some significance as a choice of date for the terms of office to commence.

Nowadays, there are seven Stewards of the Club. Five are elected to serve for three years, while the Senior Steward and his deputy are elected for a four-year term.

However, when Sir Charles Bunbury became Steward in 1768 it was a solitary appointment. Bunbury was the ideal Turf administrator for the time.

Born near Newmarket at Great Barton, where his father had been the vicar, he was interested in politics, supporting Whig philosophies and very much a disciple of his fellow turfiste, Charles James Fox. He loathed the slave trade, which combined with the cotton business was enriching the Port of Liverpool, and in that curiously elegant manner which has always distinguished the English upper classes he contrived to be elected MP for Suffolk whilst abroad on the Grand Tour.

Perhaps it is fortunate that Bunbury did not have to address the voters in an election campaign, as he was not a great speaker. His maiden speech in the Commons was so stumbling and ineffectual that one fellow MP was unkind enough to suggest that Bunbury should be spelled with an 'M' rather than an 'N'. Even so, he happily represented his constituents for nearly two generations.

In the face of fierce competition which included the regal figure of King George III, in 1762 Bunbury married one of the greatest beauties of the period. His bride was Lady Sarah Lennox, daughter of the second Duke of Richmond. The first Duke was the illigitimate son of King Charles II and one of the monarch's favourite mistresses, Louise de Keroualle, known in the King's affections by the slightly unflattering soubriquette of 'Fubbs', an old English name meaning chubby.

To judge from the contemporary portrait by Vareist, Charles must have known something we don't, for the picture reveals a sleek and seductive, even sensual countenance above a slender neck.

Assuming that Lady Sarah Lennox inherited not only her grandmother's looks but also the latter's adventurous spirit, it is not surprising to find that she quickly became bored with life as the spouse of a sporting Suffolk squire and in 1767 she deserted the now Sir Charles Bunbury, who had inherited the baronetcy in 1764, and bolted to Earlstone in Berwickshire with Lord William Gordon. A duel seemed inevitable until 'friends' of Bunbury told him that Gordon was only the latest of a sequence of admirers entertained by Lady Sarah while Sir Charles enjoyed the pleasures of the field.

Settling for divorce, Bunbury later remarried, but was childless at his death in 1821. After the affair with Gordon petered out, Lady Sarah married the Hon. George Napier and mothered three generals, one of whom, Sir Charles, became Commander in Chief in India while his brother, Sir William, wrote the definitive history of the Peninsular War.

Meanwhile Bunbury, dull husband and duller politician, was exercising a strong influence on the Turf. The age at which racehorses were expected to compete was slowly being reduced from the long accepted age of five to include four-year-olds in 1727 and three-year-olds by 1756.

The racing of juveniles was inevitable and in 1770 Bunbury and his fellow Stewards Lord Bolingbroke and Mr J. Shafto produced an order in the *Calendar* as below:

It was resolved that the Stewards should appoint some proper person to examine every colt and filly, being at the age of two, three and four years, at the ending-post, immediately after running for the first time and that the said appointed person is to sign a certificate of such examination and his opinion thereon, which certificate is to be hung up before eight o'clock in the evening of the said day of running, in the Coffee House in Newmarket.

Although the main thrust of his directive is clear, the instruction itself did not legalise two-year-old racing, as horses then took their age from 1st May and not 1st January as now. A two-year-old running in, say, March in 1771 would be regarded as a three-year-old today.

As it happened, the two-year-old Gibscutski had already blazed the trail on Newmarket Heath when defeating a six-year-old mare giving three stone in a six furlong match for 200 guineas staged on the Rowley course in 1769.

By 1773 juvenile horses were being subjected to stupidly cruel matches over four miles to which the supposed liberal humanitarian Charles James Fox was a party, but at the same November Newmarket meeting Bunbury and his fellow Stewards devised an all aged event over an extended two miles. This race, the Grosvenor Plate, set two-year-olds to carry 4st 8lb, three-year-olds 6st 7lb, four-year-olds 7st 9lb, five-year-olds 8st 5lb, six-year-olds 8st 9lb and aged horses were allotted 8st 10lb.

Probably the distance was still too far for the two-year-olds even with the massive weight concession. At all events, no juveniles took part and, other than one match race, there was no organised two-year-old racing at Newmarket until 1776, when a disappointing field of only three runners contested a sweepstake.

Bunbury and his colleagues persevered, despite the apparent lack of interest, and following the inaugural July Stakes in 1786, juvenile racing became part of the sport and the progress of the thoroughbred. Many thought otherwise as some do now, blaming the racing of precocious two-year-olds for a weakening of the breed which should not have been encouraged by the Club.

Perhaps – and there is no doubt that many juveniles are over-raced by owners seeking quick returns whose interest in the Turf is financial rather than sporting. But it is the duty of any racing body to provide opportunities for all participants and the fast maturing horse should have its events, albeit minor, along with the cosseted classic candidate.

Certainly, the July Stakes has stood the test of time over two centuries, including a wartime substitute race at Windsor. The original conditions set colts to carry 8st 2lb, fillies 8st, with any horse by Eclipse or Highflyer 3 pounds extra. It was not designed as a classic test, although some notable names did go on, including The Flying Dutchman and Sceptre.

Regrettably, the cruel and pointless practice of racing yearlings followed in the wake of legitimate juvenile events and the Club inexplicably allowed this to happen, an indifference for which they have been strongly criticised and rightly so.

The yearling course was over two furlongs and 147 yards and the first match took place at the Houghton meeting in 1771. The effect on horses only just over 12 months old often matched against their seniors albeit with huge weight concessions, can only be imagined. Charles James Fox again illustrated that his liberalism towards his fellow men did not extend to his fellow creatures, racing Sister of Gold as a yearling and she went on to be a fine broodmare. Indeed, it seems that it was the distaff side which survived the better. A filly called Little Lady won fifteen races after scoring as a yearling at Shrewsbury, later becoming the dam of 2,000 guineas winner Camballo. Luckily, yearling racing never attracted the interest of the public and was thankfully abolished by the Jockey Club in 1859.

Bunbury's reign was long and productive but, until the infamous Escape affair in 1791, the authority of the Jockey Club was unproven in absolute terms.

Although it was important that minor miscreants on the Heath and those who ran their horses to cheat fellow owners and the public alike were dealt with promptly and effectively, Bunbury knew that he needed a big fish of which to make an example; and who bigger or better than H.R.H. The Prince of Wales.

The First Gentleman of Europe had been a member of the Club since, as Robert Black put it, 'the moment he arrived at the age of indiscretion'. The Prince's initial period of activity on the Turf between 1784 and 1786, came to an ignominious end when he simply ran out of money. In its wisdom, Parliament released him from further embarrassment by paying his bills and increasing his income. Perhaps H.R.H. was lucky in that the Prime Minister, William Pitt the Younger, was a member of a family described as 'decidedly horsey'.

At all events, the Prince resumed his racing career, aided and literally abetted by his jockey, the dandyish Sam Chifney Snr. Chifney's sartorial flamboyance and artistry in the saddle was only matched by a duplicity which would have made Machiavelli sob with envy; and, as the latter remarked, 'A prince who wants to hold his own must know how to do wrong when necessary.'

The Prince and Chifney were heavy gamblers, and it followed that both the opportunity and the necessity were never far away and very close to home at Newmarket on Thursday, 20th October, 1791. The Royal runner in a four horse event was the six-year-old Escape, generally considered to be one of the best colts in training. Naturally enough, Escape was a hot favourite at 2/1 on to beat the other contenders Coriander, Skylark and Pipator. The distance was two miles.

To the chagrin of his supporters, Escape finished last of the quartet, the winner being Coriander at 4/1. Since odds-on favourites do get beaten from time to time the matter might have been dismissed as a case of 'that's racing', but for Escape being pulled out again the following day.

This time there were six runners. Pipator, third in the original race, and Skylark, second to Coriander, again took the field with Chanticleer the well-backed favourite at 7/4. The distance had doubled to four miles. Escape, easy in the market at 5/1 from 4/1 not only defeated Chanticleer, but completely reversed the form of the previous day with Skylark and Pipator, scoring an easy victory.

Bunbury and the other Stewards of the Jockey Club, Mr Thomas Panton and Mr Ralph Dutton, summoned Chifney to account for this somewhat in-and-out running. The rider explained that Escape was a stuffy horse who needed the race 'to clear his pipes' on the Thursday, and accordingly had not backed his mount, but he did admit to having twenty guineas (about £7,500 in modern terms) on Escape for Friday's four-miler.

It must be remembered that jockeys were allowed to bet at the time, and the scale of the wager did not surprise the Stewards, but they did not believe a word of the excuses for Thursday's debacle and, given Chifney's past record,

Turfites of the period as seen by Rowlandson. This incidentally, shows the type of whip outlawed by the Jockey Club.

were unlikely to do so. Bunbury went to the Prince and informed him that no gentleman would start against him as long as he employed Chifney.

The more the matter is investigated, the murkier it looks. Chifney was in debt to the tune of £300 to a certain Mr Vauxhall Clarke, who laid Chifney's twenty guineas as Lake, the Prince's racing manager, refused to place the commission on behalf of the jockey, adding enigmatically if ungrammatically, 'No, I will have nothing to do with it, there are so many unpleasant things happen.'

Apart from any other consideration, the affair was a perfect example of why jockeys were eventually prohibited from betting. Chefney may have stopped Escape on the Thursday to oblige Mr Vauxhall Clarke, thus clearing his £300 debt and enabling the bookmaker to lay the horse safe in the knowledge that it could not win. Meanwhile Chifney could back his rivals, and allegedly won £700 in the process.

Quite how the Prince was implicated in the Thursday race is uncertain. Chifney's account says that the Prince thought Escape was sure to win and although the jockey tried to put the owner off he stopped short of actually saying that the horse was not fit. The Prince then ordered Chifney to make the running, an instruction which the rider ignored.

However, we have only Chifney's word to rely on and he may have been 'economical with the truth'. The Prince apparently claimed later not to have had 'a striver' on Escape on Thursday, which is odd if he was so certain of victory, and it is unlikely that he did not take advantage of the horse's chances on the Friday, chances doubtless revealed by Chifney at the inevitable post race discussion the day before. To be fair to the Prince of Wales he stood by Chifney and disposed of his stud and stock, withdrawing from Newmarket altogether and in effect warning himself off.

The Escape Affair. Chifney was warned off by the Jockey Club Stewards who intimated to the Prince that if he rode again no gentleman would ride against him. Here Chifney's horse is hobbled by a banner featuring the royal motto. The Prince stood by him and gave him a pension.

Of course, the Stewards could simply have warned-off Chifney and allowed the Prince to continue. After all, to this day owners require no licence and are generally presumed to be innocent in such affairs unless it is proven otherwise, in which case they are 'excluded'.

By giving the Prince a choice of action, Bunbury may have been showing due deference to royalty. On the other hand, even to threaten such a personage with exclusion demonstrated the growing power and prestige of the Club, although the impact would not have been as great if the Prince had sacked Chifney and continued with the sport he undoubtedly loved. As it was, the Prince rose to the bait and Bunbury landed the big fish he needed.

Fourteen years later, when Chifney was languishing in the Fleet prison for debt and where he was to die in 1807, the Club issued a grovelling message to the Prince asking him to return to Newmarket. His Royal Highness promised to patronise the Heath again, but never did, preferring the delights of Ascot and Brighton. The Prince was wise; at Newmarket he would have been a 'watched pot' as more than one 'warm' jockey turned trainer could testify.

Anthony St. Leger devised the world's first classic race won by an unnamed horse, later called Alabaculia and owned by Lord Rochester.

When Bunbury died in 1821 he had seen the innovation of all five classic races. He probably had some influence on the founding of the St Leger in 1776, although as with the other major classics, it was the work of an unofficial committee rather than one individual.

The St Leger belongs to Col. Anthony St Leger, properly pronounced 'Sellinger', Lord Rockingham and General 'Johnny' Burgoyne; the Oaks to the 12th Earl of Derby and Burgoyne and the Derby to Lord Derby and Burgoyne again, Bunbury, Charles James Fox and Richard Brinsley Sheridan. The Guineas races can be attributed to Bunbury and his fellow Stewards of the time.

Much nonsense has been written about the circumstances surrounding the naming of the premier classic, the most popular theory being that a toss of the coin decided between Derby and Bunbury. This defies the social conventions of the period and the race would have been named after the host unless he demurred, as Rockingham did at the St Leger dinner.

Bunbury found compensation when he won the inaugural Derby with Diomed but it would have been more appropriate if the most famous race in the world had been named after the first great administrator of the Turf.

No doubt he took this disappointment like the sporting gentleman he had been throughout a life not entirely free of the 'slings and arrows of outrageous fortune'. Little is known of the private person, although he was said to have been tight-fisted in rewarding his servants. The example most frequently quoted is the £30 tip given to his jockey Tom Goodisson after he had won the

Derby on Bunbury's Smolensko in 1813. Sir Charles's excuse for this poor reward was that his bookmaker Brograve had welshed and then killed himself.

Quite why Bunbury was betting on races in which he might well have been required to adjudicate is another matter, but given that £30 in the early 19th century would be worth £10,500 today and that Goodisson was free to back his mount, perhaps the jockey was not so hard done by.

Undoubtedly Sir Charles behaved correctly when offered £2,000 by a travelling showman to exhibit Smolensko up and down the country. The offer was firmly refused and some might wish that the owners of some retired champions would show the same consideration today.

After forty years at the top of Turf affairs, Bunbury left the sport with a ruling body whose authority was unchallenged, a structure of appointed starters, judges, clerks of the scales and other officials, and the Jockey Club could boast a membership of rather more integrity than in 'Louse' Pigott's day. The bookmaker had also started to make his presence felt, and since the layers were to play a large role in subsequent racing affairs, it would be appropriate to take a look at the activities of the early bookmakers before moving on to the next era of racing administration, presided over by Lord George Bentinck.

CHAPTER 4

The Bookies and their Bettors

At the time of the Jockey Club's emergence in the early 1750s gambling was confined to owners and stable 'connections' betting against each other, but there was no reason why the public should not do likewise if they could find someone to accommodate them. As with so many of the more agreeable aspects of English life, taverns were the obvious rendezvous for such negotiations and it soon became necessary for an eager punter to seek out a person willing to lay bets against more than one runner in a race.

To record the bets and control the odds in such a way as to make a profit, the layer had to keep a book. He also had to be literate and numerate, implying a standard of education in late-eighteenth-century England mostly confined to doctors, lawyers and clergymen.

The Lord Chief Justice flogs Lady Buckinghamshire for flouting the Gaming Laws with two more miscreants in the pillory.

The Betting Post by Rowlandson in 1789 where wagers were struck by mounted punters in the days before the Book had taken over. The Prince of Wales is on the left and on the right with his crutches is Major O'Kelly, owner of Eclipse.

It was unlikely that you could have struck a wager in Harley Street, the Temple or the crypt of Westminster Abbey, but you would have had no difficulty at Tyburn in Hyde Park, where the punter had a choice of odds chalked on blackboards or fixed to trees and could amuse himself with the spectacle of public executions.

However, public betting was illegal and soon the bookies and punters were back in the drinking dens, mostly around Fleet Street. The gentry were not too proud to frequent these unsalubrious establishments. Since they preferred to settle their accounts weekly, and more importantly at indisputable odds, the starting price system came into being. The first newspaper to publish starting prices was the *Evening News* in 1883. The editor was Frank Harris, once described by his sometime friend Oscar Wilde as 'every other inch a gentleman'.

This reflection on Harris's character was amply borne out when he telegraphed Wilde from the South of France, 'Please send an Old Etonian tie.' Wilde complied, only to receive another message two days later. This missive read, 'Please send old Harrovian tie.'

Notwithstanding Harris's dubious reputation, the system worked and Starting Price returns remain the bedrock of betting on horse racing today.

Meanwhile the old aristos and Jockey Club members had their own gambling facilities, notably at the ubiquitous auctioneer Richard Tattersall's Subscription Rooms at Hyde Park Corner, William Crockford's gambling saloon in

Crockford the Shark by Rowlandson. Described as a really evil man, he started up in St. James's Street but had interests in several other gaming houses in the area. He soon moved his attentions to Newmarket which became his 'second home' with a big house, 50 acres and a stud of horses, but his fortunes on the turf waned and he went back to gaming houses. Eventually however he is reputed to have been responsible for making bookmaking a respectable profession.

Newmarket High Street or the former fishmonger's eponymous establishment in St James's Street.

Crockford enjoyed more notoriety at the time, but it was the name of Tattersall which survived. The Tattersalls Ring on every racecourse remembers the period when it was an enclosure used by bookmakers and punters who were members of the two guineas a year subscription rooms at Tattersall's London premises.

The Jockey Club were not interested in betting as such, acting only to ensure that the Rules of Racing were fair to all concerned and that debts of honour were settled, as gambling accounts were and remain unenforceable by law. Accordingly Tattersalls Committee was formed in 1886 to settle betting disputes and to report all defaulters. The committee operated and continues to exist under the authorisation of the Jockey Club, to whom the committee is still responsible. Any person posted as a defaulter by Tattersalls Committee is automatically warned off until the debt is discharged.

The ubiquitous Richard Tattersall, son of a north country yeoman, became the head of the world's first and greatest firm of blood-stock auctioneers. He let out rooms for Jockey Club meetings and owned the champion racehorse Highflyer.

The idea that betting should in any way contribute to the funding of racing did not cross the collective mind of the Jockey Club between 1790 when a Mr Ogden was the first known public bookmaker and the late 1950s when the Betting and Gaming Act was going through Parliament. In the latter instance, this amiable indifference resulted in the loss of a golden opportunity to put the sport on a firm financial footing forever and the wholly inadequate betting levy was the only crumb saved from the table.

However, the bookmaking fraternity were to play a large if not always honourable role in the affairs of nineteenth-century racing, as we shall see in an examination of the career of Lord George Bentinck.

He was born in 1802, the third son of the fourth Duke of Portland. Racing administration was clearly in Lord George's blood as the Duke, a member of the Jockey Club for well over fifty years, not only supplied the cash for the Club to buy the freehold of the Coffee Room, the new rooms

Bentinck, son of the Duke of Portland, took over the reins from Bunbury. He was a countrified and refined English gentleman yet with a cool and calculating intellect which made him an effective scourge of wrongdoers.

and the adjacent land in 1831, but was the owner of a large expanse of Newmarket Heath. In 1820 he put in hand immense work at his own expense to secure the town as an unrivalled centre for racing. Acres of scrub land were laid to grass, and territory bordering on the Heath was purchased to protect the gallops from those possibly hostile to the sport.

By bringing an action for trespass against a Mr S. Hawkins at Cambridge Assizes in 1827, the Duke established finally and forever the right of the Jockey Club to warn persons off Newmarket Heath, the Club producing evidence to show that it had proprietorship of the Heath as tenants of His Grace the Duke of Portland since 1753.

As an owner the Duke achieved poor reward, his sole classic success being the 1819 Derby which he won with Tiresias. He did not bet and despised the habit in others, an aversion which his son Lord George found onerous and cramping to his style.

Portland was sensible enough to realise that the noise of the racecourse would upset the thoroughbred. The racket on most tracks is bad enough today with the racegoers ears constantly battered by often needless announcements over public address systems broadcast at a high decibel level, but in the early nineteenth-century the punters thought it a fine thing to drop a squib under a runner's tail.

The Duke familiarised his animals accordingly, much in the same way as police horses are trained now. It was said that a creature which survived the treatment would not look up from its feed if a pistol went off behind it.

Lord George Bentinck came into racing as an owner and gambler on a considerable scale and after the usual early disasters was very successful in both spheres. As his father dispised betting, Bentinck's loss of £26,000 over the 1826 St Leger did not go down too well at the family seat of Welbeck.

The Duke decided to give his errant son an estate in Ayrshire in the pious but mistaken hope that this would engage Bentinck's attentions away from the racecourse, although refusing to bail him out of debt; this had to be done by the Duchess and her daughter. Cheerfully allowing the Ayrshire lands to manage without him, Bentinck persuaded his brothers Lord Tichfield and Lord Henry Bentinck to open an account for him at Drummond's Bank to a limit of £300,000. As this sum would be worth about seventy million in modern terms, Lord George was not exactly strapped for cash when he embarked on his career on the Turf.

An arrogant man, he offended many people, ultimately including Charles Greville, his cousin and fellow member of the Jockey Club, who said of Bentinck, 'He feared no man and did nothing by halves.'

Greville was later to find this all too true when they quarrelled bitterly over the running of a filly called Preserve – but in the early years Bentinck needed him. To avoid the wrath of his father, Lord George ran his horses in Greville's name along with other catspaws including Lord Orford, Lord Lichfield and even a Doncaster publican named Bowe. Whilst purporting to be the Duke of Richmond's 'manager-man', as Robert Black would have it, he also ran his horses in the Duke's name until Bentinck's too obvious interest in the Duchess's unquestioned charms caused His Grace to tell Lord George to move his string elsewhere 'as it had become too large' for Goodwood, the Duke's Sussex estate.

As Goodwood by then extended to 17,000 acres, the excuse might have seemed a little transparent except to one of Bentinck's insensitivity. Anyway, he was in too good a position to care; gambles such as the touch on Elis in the 1836 St Leger, when Bentinck had constructed a horse box which took Elis to Doncaster in a faster time than it would have taken the horse to walk, the common practice. The bookmakers, hearing that Elis was still in his Sussex stable ten days before the race, laid Lord George 12/1 to his money, believing that the horse could never get to Doncaster in time.

In fact Elis arrived two days prior to the St Leger and duly beat the 6/4 favourite Scroggins. Although winning enough to take advantage of the layer's duplicity, Bentinck realised that where bookmakers went greed, corruption and cheating would follow, a situation which he met head-on in 1844.

The feared Bentinck from a sketch by the Count d'Orsay. At the time of taking over as dictator of the Turf he was also being considered as a candidate for Prime Minister.

First past the post in the Derby of that year was Running Rein, owned by Mr A.W. Wood and ridden by S. Mann, 'winning' by three-quarters of a length from Orlando, owned by Colonel Jonathan Peel and ridden by Nat Flatman who in 1848 became the first jockey to be recorded as champion.

'Running Rein' was a ringer, actually being a four-year-old called Maccabeus, Bentinck had grave suspicions before the Derby as Maccabeus, parading as 'Running Rein', had won a two-year-old race at Newmarket in 1843. The horse was actually three and looked it.

At the instigation of Bentinck, the Duke of Rutland, who owned the runner-up, objected. Bets were settled under protest but, at the Jockey Club enquiry two weeks later, the case collapsed when the real Running Rein's stud groom confirmed that the Newmarket winner was undoubtedly his former charge. Bentinck was sure he knew otherwise and set about collecting evidence of the activities of 'Pickle' Higgins and Goodman Levy, like Higgins, a professional gambler who gave Maccabeus to his ostensible owner Wood in settlement of a forage bill.

Five days before the Derby, Bentinck, John Bowes and John Scott petitioned the Epsom stewards requesting that they should investigate Running Rein's identity and to ensure that an examination was made of the horse's mouth before the start, which would or would not confirm the animal's age based on the 'long in the tooth' theory.

Bowes, who in 1853 bred the first winner of the Triple Crown, West Australian, had a vested interest in the race, being the owner of another runner, T'Auld Square, trained by Scott. John Scott had already sent out three Derby winners and was to train two more and enjoy forty-one classic successes in all; Bentinck, Bowes and Scott were men who knew their business, but the petition was in vain. The Epsom stewards, acting on the advice of the then Captain Rous, decided that the suspect ringer should be allowed to run, but that the stakes (i.e. prize money) should be withheld pending post-race inquiries.

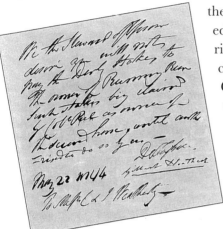

Letter to Weatherbys from the Epsom Stewards telling them to withold payment of the money due to Mr Wood pending the Running Rein inquiry.

When Maccabeus, the bogus 'Running Rein', duly passed the judge at the head of a field which it later transpired included at least one six-year-old, a favourite grossly impeded by foul riding and a well-backed runner whose 'stopping' jockey had clearly decided to travel via Leatherhead, Bentinck urged Colonel Peel to claim the Stakes on behalf of the runner-up, Orlando.

The stewards sent for Mr Wood, but not surprisingly he was nowhere to be found. The payments of 'winnings' in respect of bets, sweepstakes and lotteries were thrown into confusion, and Goodman Levy and his friends were unable to collect on 'Running Rein' at the latter's starting price of 10/1. Reputedly, the conspirators stood to win £50,000.

The Running Rein Derby the nortorious race which caused a sensation involving pullings, doping, switching, foul riding, litigation and the wrong doers fleeing the country.

Eventually the Club stood back and allowed the case to be settled by the courts. Wood sued for the stakes, opposed by Peel, but the only indisputable way to substantiate the plaintiff's claims would have been to produce 'Running Rein'. Obviously this was something which Wood could not afford to do, and he was forced to withdraw from the case, accompanied by some strong remarks from the bench when Judge Baron Alderson observed, 'If gentlemen condescend to race with blackguards, they must expect to be cheated.'

This time it was 'Gentlemen 1, Blackguards 0'. Goodman Levy, 'Pickles' Higgins and company fled the country, Orlando was awarded the race, Running Rein never ran again and died peacefully on a farm in Northamptonshire, while Lord George was given a testimonial by a grateful betting public. Bentinck never touched a penny of the money and in time the testimonial became the Bentinck Benevolent Fund, still in existence today for the benefit of trainers and jockeys and their dependants who fall on hard times.

Lord George had irritated the judge to a considerable extent during the trial, to say nothing of the plaintiff's counsel, Mr Cockburn, with his interjections and consummate knowledge of racing. Baron Alderson, who fancied himself as a racing buff but in reality was an amateur compared to Bentinck, said during his summing-up '... if gentlemen would only race with gentlemen, there would be no difficulty...'

Lord George knew that those happy days had gone forever and he was also aware that the Running Rein affair was only the tip of the iceberg, merely the most infamous racing fraud in a decade which came to be known as 'The Filthy Forties'.

The Jockey Club had been widely criticised in some quarters for backing off in the Running Rein case, whilst treating comparatively trivial offenders with a draconian mode of procedure. In 1845, as Lord George drew up fresh battle-lines to fight corruption, the Club passed a rule 'That no races for gentlemen shall be allowed at Newmarket during the regular meetings without the sanction of the Stewards, and that in the event of such sanction being obtained, these races be the first or last of the day'.

Thus, the old 'jockies' were no more able to ride against professionals by right, and the 'Jockey Club' became a misnomer, as it has remained. However the permission for amateurs to ride against professionals was to be granted frequently for many years to come.

The sport of gentlemen referred to wistfully by Judge Alderson was not the sport of the people, and Bentinck decided that they must be protected from criminals and defaulters. As one journalist observed in 1847, he 'made it his great care to provide for the masses – a portion of the company that previously had little thought or attention bestowed on their wants'.

At the time Bentinck had forty horses in training to carry his sky-blue colours and it must be certain that he acted partly from self-interest. Equally, his reforms were carried out against a social background of immense change, spearheaded by the spread of the railways and the introduction of the electric telegraph. The former, encouraged by the activities of a swindler called George Hudson, alias 'The Railway King', caused many to plunge headlong into the speculation of the 'Railwaymania', losing heavily in bogus or unsuccessful companies, while the telegram became a method of defrauding bookmakers by the means of 'after time' bets for many years.

Slavery had been abolished only eleven years earlier as had the abuse of child labour, but it was still the age of the workhouse and the Poor Law while fortunes were being made in such comodities as the pig-iron needed to build the metal-hulled ships rapidly replacing the wooden 'merchantmen'.

Inevitably, in a 'get rich quick' society, it was a time of high corruption and although Bentinck later played an important part in national politics, for the time being he confined his attentions to the parlous state of the Turf. He realised that the key was the reformation of racecourse practices. The Rules themselves were for the most part adequate, but were either being poorly administered or simply ignored.

The greatest area of laxity was at the start. It was quite common for jockeys in important races to gang up against the favourites and cause as many false starts as possible to unnerve the fancied horses and their riders, playing an elaborate game of bluff with the starter as they risked being left.

Bentinck's runners were often the victims of this gamesmanship, notably when his filly Crucifix was 3/1 on favourite for the 1840 Oaks in a field of fifteen and the start was delayed for an hour by sixteen false starts. Lord George was sanguine on that occasion, merely observing, 'She could not lose; but on the contrary, could afford to flirt with them for half a day.'

Crucifix duly won easily enough, but the starting system was ludicrous. When the horses lined up, the starter simply shouted 'Go' and, if some runners were left, had to recall the others and repeat the same process until a start was achieved.

The ultimate absurdity came at Goodwood, where the starter suffered a speech impediment which prevented him from enunciating the word 'Go' without stammering. Lord George's answer was to start many races himself, posting a flagman in full view of the jockeys some yards ahead of the field. Having literally dragooned the horses into line – he had held a commission in a cavalry regiment – Bentinck stood a little way behind the flank of the runners, out of sight from the jockeys but in full view of the flagman. When Bentinck dropped his flag, it was the signal to the flagman to do likewise, which in turn signalled the start of the race.

Any jockey attempting to come 'the old soldier' with Lord George was promptly fined £25 for each offence, but in any case few professional riders would have questioned his undoubted authority. This method of starting remained in force until the introduction of the starting gate over half a century later.

Bentinck also introduced separate enclosures on the racetrack, with facilities for racegoers depending on the charges for entry, fined the Clerk of the Course if a race did not go off on time and insisted on the runners being numbered on a racecard, complemented by a comprehensive number board in front of the stands.

He instructed that all runners were to be saddled at a specific place and paraded before the public prior to each race. The weighing-out and weighing-in processes were subject to tighter regulation and security, while the astonishing custom of the winning owner giving a present to the judge after an important event was not surprisingly abolished.

Bentinck instigated the draw for places at the start, which was performed by the jockeys who drew their respective numbers from a bag, supervised by the judge at the time of weighing-out. Thus, the jockey had no excuse for ignorance of his correct draw, which was then relayed to the starter by the

THE WEIGHING ROOM

Apart from the Bentinck cartoon below, various forms of weighing-in and out. The regulations were tightened up by Bentinck and remain a concern of the Jockey Club.

Weighing-in by J. Rowlandson. In the 18th century horses were raced in heats and the jockeys were weighed and the horses scraped down during the half hour rest between them.

Below left, the weighing room at Epsom in 1933 by Isaac Cullin.

Frankie Dettori, flat champion jockey in 1994 and 1995, weighing-out at Sandown Park.

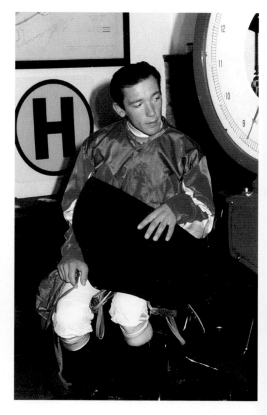

judge. Any jockey starting from the wrong place was fined a fiver. The starter also had the authority to order the rider of a restive or vicious horse to drop out of his place and start on the extreme outside of the field.

The number boards which displayed the number of the winning horse, once the judge's decision was known, were a particular boon to punters, as hitherto some bookmakers had been in the habit of deciding which runner to pay out on, depending on the scale of their liabilities.

If all of these reforms seem commonplace to the modern racegoer, it is a tribute to Bentinck's remarkable forward-thinking.

Thinking ahead is a mental capacity shared by all great men and women, and essential for the successful politician. Lord George had been a Member of Parliament since the age of twenty-six, taking his duties lightly and treating the Commons as a club to frequent after a day's hunting. He did not make his maiden speech for eight years, but in 1846 the Tory Prime Minister Sir Robert Peel, brother of the gallant colonel who owned Orlando, decided to repeal the Corn Laws following the failure of the Irish potato crop in 1845-46. Peel supported free trade but was opposed by those members of his own party who wished to protect English farmers by keeping the taxes on imported corn.

The disaffected Tories, lead by Bentinck and Benjamin Disraeli, broke away to form their own Protectionist Party. Promptly selling all his racing stock and his stud to the Hon. Edward Mostyn for £10,000 to include the services of Kitchener, his diminutive jockey who had the distinction of winning the Chester Cup in 1844 on Lord George's Red Deer carrying 4 stone, Bentinck threw himself into politics with all the vigour which had marked his pursuit of villains on the Turf.

It was not an easy take and just before the Derby in 1848, on 22nd and 24th May, the Parliamentary Committee dealing with the repeal act had failed to approve Bentinck's resolutions in favour of colonial interest. A further blow was to come on Derby Day. Surplice, which he had bred and sold to Edward Mostyn, won the premier classic in which Bentinck had never gained victory despite a lifelong ambition.

As he was standing, clouded in gloom before the bookshelves in the Commons library, he was interrupted by Disraeli wearing the blue sash of the Garter on his breast. Asked the reason for the despair, Bentinck explained, adding, 'All my life I have been waiting for this, and for what have I sacrificed it? You do not know what the Derby is.' 'Yes I do,' replied Disraeli smoothing his sash, 'it is the Blue Ribbon of the Turf.' 'It is the Blue Ribbon of the Turf,' repeated Bentinck, as he sat down at a table and buried himself in a folio of statistics.

But a few days later on Monday, 29th May when the Commons carried his resolution in favour of a ten shilling differential duty for the colonies at the last moment and by virtue of his own casting vote, it was another story.

'We have saved the colonies,' Bentinck triumphantly declared. 'I know that it must be so. It is the knell of Free Trade.'

It seemed that a glittering political career was before him but, four months later, strained by strict dieting and overwork, he was found dead on the estate at Welbeck. He had suffered a heart attack while walking the six mile journey to Thoresby, the seat of Lord Manners, where he was to spend a few days. He was only forty-six years of age.

Lord George was something of a humbug and like many great men tended to think that rules were for other people. He certainly was not above pulling a few strokes on the racecourse to ensure the success of the gambling operations needed to sustain his vast racing interests, but as Charles Greville observed, Bentinck justified these stratagems to himself as part of his own peculiar code of morality and honour.

He could, again in the manner of some successful people, be vain, arrogant, domineering, ruthless and unkind; after all, you do not achieve greatness in public life by patting children on the head and handing around scones at tea parties. A man who owed Bentinck £4,000 in losing wagers, having explained that he could not settle in full, offered £2,000 and the balance in instalments.

Settling Day at Tattersalls by James Pollard 1835. Tattersalls' horse sales was set up in the late 18th century and let some apartments, with chef and wine cellar, for the Jockey Club as well as the famous subscription rooms for members to lay bets. The ring was organised after a further Tattersalls expansion in 1818 and here ring members can be seen sitting at tables and walking around giving and receiving bills. Behind can be seen the door to the subscription rooms.

'Sir,' replied Lord George, 'no man has the right to bet if he cannot pay should he lose. The sum I want off you is £4,000; and until that is paid, you are in the list of defaulters in the ring and on the course.'

Bentinck won only seven classic races, including the St Leger won by Elis in the colours of Lord Lichfield, and most were trained by John Barham Day at Danebury in Hampshire, where he sent his horses after the difference with the Duke of Richmond. Perhaps a small reward for his efforts, but his career on the Turf was comparatively short and his legacy to future racing administration was beyond any valuation.

CHAPTER 5

The Admiral in Command

When the then Captain Rous advised the Epsom stewards in the Running Rein affair, he had been a member of the Jockey Club for twenty-three years. Born at Henham Hall, Suffolk, in 1795, Henry John Rous was the son of Sir John Rous who became the Earl of Stradbroke. On the death of the first Earl, the title passed to Rous's elder brother who by coincidence was one of the stewards serving at Epsom on that infamous day in 1844.

Educated at Westminster, Rous joined the Navy and at the age of fourteen sailed in H.M.S. *Victory*. Later he served with distinction in Bacchante, commanding a yawl in the Mediterranean and steering his craft through heavy grapeshot and musketry fire to board several enemy gunboats. It was 1813, and Rous was still only eighteen years old.

Commissioned as Lieutenant the following year, he was elevated to Post-Captain in 1822 and took command of His Majesty's frigate *Rainbow* in 1825. Rous spent the next three years sailing around India, Australia and New Holland. While in port at Sydney, he organised both horse racing and cock fighting, and when the *Rainbow* was paid off in 1830, he spent the next few years on half-pay at Newmarket studying the sport in general and in particular the Rules of Racing, in which he was to become the greatest expert.

1835 saw his pennant fly again, this time from the thirty-six ton frigate *Pique*. In the autumn, he set sail from Quebec for England. The ship was driven by high winds on to a sunken reef off the coast of Labrador and stuck fast for eleven hours.

Finally floating off, Rous was faced with the task of steering an almost rudderless command with no keel and two sprung masts with 1,500 miles of Atlantic Ocean between him and Spithead. The voyage took twenty days, navigation not aided by the leaking vessel shipping two feet of water an hour.

Rous was exonerated at the inevitable court martial which followed and although receiving the admiration of his naval colleagues, his feat of seamanship was only grudgingly acknowledged by the Lords of the Admiralty.

Accordingly, the disillusioned sailor left the service in 1836 to marry a rich wife and later become M.P. for Westminster.

The Navy's loss was racing's gain. Rous had dabbled on the Turf since 1821 when he ran a small stud with his brother Stradbroke. According to 'Thormanby', the nom-de-plume of Sydenham Dixon, 'his naval duties prevented him from paying much attention to sport on land until 1830.'

In 1840, Rous was appointed private handicapper to the 7th Duke of Bedford, with a free hand to make matches for the Duke's runners. He stood to win a quarter of the stakes and his skills netted him at least £1,500 a year from this source.

Rous ran a few horses himself until 1844, having been elected a Steward of the Jockey Club in 1838, winning some small races and his fair share of matches, but nothing of consequence. Nonetheless Rous found the Turf more to his taste than politics and resigned his Parliamentary seat in 1846.

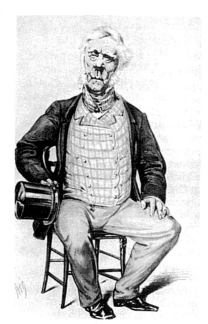

The redoubtable Honourable Admiral Henry Rous, younger son of the Earl of Stradbroke, Dictator of the Turf and father of handicapping.

In his capacity as a Steward of the Jockey Club, he became the 'nuts and bolts' man as opposed to the flamboyant reforming zeal of Bentinck. Rous found the Club to be seriously embarrassed financially, the revenue from the lands at Newmarket amounting to no more than £3,000 per annum. When he died in 1877, the income had risen to £18,000 p.a.

But his prime interests were handicapping and the Rules, and his detestation of villainy was only matched by Bentinck's. As a handicapper he was supreme, believing that 'every great handicap offers a premium to fraud, for horses are constantly started without any intention of winning, merely to hoodwink the handicapper.' It took a clever man to deceive Rous, who handicapped the match at York in 1851 between The Flying Dutchman and Voltigeur. The Flying Dutchman was set to concede eight-and-a-half pounds over two miles and ran out the winner by an official length which in fact was slightly less.

He was an inveterate correspondent in the columns of the press, and in one such epistle declared, 'I have been looking out for thirty years for the phenomenon (public handicapper) without success. I might pick out three Prime Ministers, who would satisfy the public, but I can discover no man gifted with the qualifications of the handicapper.

'We want a man, like Caesar's wife, above suspicion, of independent means, a perfect knowledge of the form and actual condition of every public horse, without having the slightest interest in any stable. If by any possibility you can find this man above price, he would then throw up his office in three months, disgusted with many horse owners, whose sole knowledge of racing is confined to running horses for stakes, and abusing the handicappers.'

As his description of this paragon fitted Rous like a glove, he decided to brave the wrath of disgruntled owners and accepted the post of Public Handicapper in 1855. The racegoers were delighted. Rous was by now nearly sixty, but his physique was unimpaired, doubtless a legacy of his seafaring days, and his knowledge of form, constantly updated by much burning of the midnight oil, was unrivalled.

Fair minded to the point of pedantry, he was in attendance at every important race meeting, armed with his huge naval telescope which gave him a close-up of the runners at any stage of the race, even on the vast expanse of Newmarket Heath.

His custom was to examine every runner in the paddock, watch the race from the top of the stand, and then return to the unsaddling area as quickly as he could to see which of the runners was blowing. On the Rowley Mile at Newmarket he varied this routine by observing the race from the Bushes which he reckoned to be the ideal vantage point for detecting non-triers.

Any offending jockey would receive a choice selection of nautical phrases from Rous as the wretched rider passed by, leaving him in no doubt that the subterfuge had been spotted and would find its way into Rous's ever-present notebook.

He was equally stringent on the training grounds, missing very little of the work, details of which all went into the book.

This latter exercise would be unthinkable today, and pointless anyway. Racing is by no means free of chicanery in the late twentieth century but considerably more so than in Rous's time. Trials on the gallops are now the exception rather than a daily practice and the information available would be scanty, while the strict monitoring of public form in the age of computers and videos assists handicappers far more than peering through binoculars on windswept heaths and foggy downs.

But Rous, like Bentinck, was a man who did what he thought was right at the time. Both boosted the lot of the punter; Bentinck with his detailed information, and Rous with his precise handicapping.

It matters not that owners and trainers complained about their horse's rating; they do so today, and always will. No handicapper allots weights on the basis of the trainer's standing in the racing world, but a trainer's past record might be worthy of consideration.

The bookies' tout Daniel Dawson was hanged in 1811 for poisoning a number of horses at Newmarket – an extreme pre-doping tactic on behalf of unscrupulous bookies.

Rous's London residence was in Berkeley Square and either by accident or design Fred Swindell moved in next door. Mr Swindell was a bookmaker who's views on punters agreed with the philosophies of Phineas Barnum, a contemporary, and Sam Goldwyn fifty year later.

The great showman Barnum always asserted, 'There's a sucker born every minute' – and film mogul Goldwyn averred, 'Never over-estimate the intelligence of the public.' Swindell improved on Barnum with his remark, 'A mug is born every minute, and thank Gawd some of 'em live.' He went on to anticipate Goldwyn's theory with, 'I 'ates people as loses watches. Give me a man who can pinch one when times is bad.'

Modern bookmakers are far too conscious of public relations to make such observations today, but the kernel of truth remains. At all events it was not to Swindell's disadvantage to take note of Rous's aristocratic callers, many doubtless members of the Jockey Club, on the day prior to the publication of the weights for an important handicap.

ON THE

LAWS AND PRACTICE

OF

HORSE RACING,

ETC., ETC.,

BY

THE HONOURABLE CAPTAIN ROUS, R.N.

LONDON:

PUBLISHED BY BAILY, BROTHERS,
ROYAL EXCHANGE BUILDINGS, CORNHILL.

1850.

Rous's influential book.

While Bentinck looked to an enforcement of the Rules, Rous considered their refinement and practical application. His book, *The Laws and Practice of Horse-Racing*, published in 1850, was definitive at the time and many elements are still relevant. The book preambles with a brief history of the English thoroughbred which is not very complimentary to Arab strains. This is followed by a concise explanation of the Newmarket Rules of Racing, as they were then known, followed by equally cogent descriptions of the duties of racecourse officials, starters, judges, clerks of the course, etc., and concludes with a brilliantly analysed and extremely entertaining catalogue of 'Difficult Judgements' which could well have been included by A.P. Herbert in the hilarious *Misleading Cases,* with the exception that in this instance the stories were all true.

The book was brought up-to-date in a second volume published in 1866. This work included essays *On the State of the English Turf, On the State of the Law, On the Rules of Racing, On Starting – Riding Races – Jockeys* and *On the Rules of Betting,* together with an exhaustive summary of more case-law to cover the repetition of such unlikely eventualities as both jockeys falling during a match and both horses contesting a match being brought down by a man employed to clear the course, causing the death of one of the runners.

To say that Rous's views, not only on racing but on his fellow men, were jaundiced is to put it mildly. However, this sourness was not without good reason. For instance, he points out in the second volume that the 'get-rich-quick' society described in Chapter Four had prospered to the extent that the number of horses in training had doubled since 1826 to a figure of 2,500, but except at such venues as Ascot and Newmarket where the Turf was 'protected by gentlemen' owners were being cheated by unscrupulous clerks-of-the-course at the gaff tracks, Brighton receiving particular mention.

The top courses do not escape criticism either. Doncaster had increased its revenue from £4,000 per annum to £7,000 in ten years, but put up only £1,200 in prize money with no increase over the period and still expected the winner of the Great Yorkshire Stakes to return £50 in 'expenses' from a prize of £200 and the winner of the Doncaster Stakes to return £20 from £100.

These sums, ostensibly to pay for policing and officials, were in fact levied

Doncaster – the breeding ground for roguery.

many times over and furthermore the winner was penalised for future races on the basis of £100 rather than £80. This contrasted badly with the profits accruing to Doncaster over ten years which amounted to £50,000 and Rous's point was well made.

At a time when the use or misuse of the whip continues to make headlines in the sporting press, it is interesting to reflect on Rous's words of nearly 130 years ago.

> I have never seen worse riding than amongst the young crack jockeys this autumn. Three great races were thrown away by a celebrated young jockey, because he could not wait; and he would flog his horse. These boys forget to keep a reserve; if you order them to wait till the last moment, up they go 100 yards from home, take the lead and the patient jockey hunts him down and wins by a head. Thousands of races are won by a judicious pull, and hundreds are lost by the abuse of whip and spur.

Rous did not have a very high opinion of jockeys. While Sir Nöel Coward always maintained that their brains were too close to their bottoms, and Roger Mortimer reckoned that spoiled jockeys were like spoiled children, Rous believed that they should be kept to their station, and one that was pretty far down the line. Although he was courteous to riders he did not regard them as social equals, and considered that excessive financial rewards in the form of presents from owners combined with glutinous public idolatry turned young heads and an indulgence in vanity resulted in a frame of mind where:

> They flatter themselves they are very clever and have arrived at the top of the tree when they have only reached the lower branches. The result is, they cease to listen to good advice; they ride according to their own fancy,

and the first indication of their worthlessness is rolling about on their saddles and flourishing their whips, instead of sitting still and keeping their horses by the head.

Plus ça change... some might say, and jockeys then as now are not cheap to employ. The fees were £5.5s for winning, £3.3s for a losing ride and £2.2s for riding in a private trial. The unofficial rate, not sanctioned by the Jockey Club, for a ride in the Derby, the Oaks or the St Leger was £25 and the value of the pound in 1866 would equal £120 today. Perhaps one may suppose that some contemporary jockeys might be offered an unofficial £3,000 for a classic ride – who knows?

Rous's views on 'the late Lord George Bentinck' are interesting. Discussing Bentinck's starting system, he writes:

Invested with full power to fine and suspend, he had no difficulty in starting a large field in a half-mile race. He laid down a rule that the evidence of the jockey was not to be listened to, and the statement of the starter not be contradicted. The theory was unconstitutional, but in practice it worked well; his success was perfect: the present situation of racing affairs differs widely from that of 1845. The number of races and the fields of horses have increased 30 per cent... so much therefore the greater necessity for stern discipline and speedy justice.

On the other hand, starters on provincial racecourses were 'respectable men, but notoriously incapable'.

Well, they wouldn't get away with such comments and suggestions today, but Rous and Bentinck were no-nonsense men of their time and the standards of the sport we enjoy now owe much to them.

When Bentinck abruptly gave up the Turf in 1846, racing was expanding at an almost uncontrollable rate. In the period between 1845 and 1849, twenty-five new meetings were founded, and during the next five years this figure rose to forty-three. In the decade of the 1860s, nearly a hundred new tracks appeared.

Naturally, many survived little longer than the mayfly, most collapsing within five years and few lasting for ten. Of the 186 meetings founded between 1845 and 1869, only forty-three were extant in the 1870s.

This Southsea Bubble of activity on the Turf was the combined result of the spread of the railways and greater prosperity for the country. The real value of incomes rose quite sharply in the 1840s and in the 1860s the increase was 10% up on the previous decade. There were plenty of people about who had the time to spend what is known in the modern jargon as 'the leisure pound'. Admittedly, the industrial workers had their noses to a relentless grindstone, but others had ample opportunity to amuse themselves.

The ports boasted a high proportion of casual 'dockies'; 'outwork' or working from home still operated in small manufacturing industries; self-employed craftsmen such as carpenters or cobblers arranged their own schedule of work and above all agriculture, with its seasonal working pattern, remained the principal employer.

From the time of Bentinck's retirement until Rous effectively took control in the mid-1850s, much of Lord George's work was in danger of being undone. For nearly a decade, the Club was without a man able to sustain its hard won authority, a task not made easier by the racecourses themselves. The enclosure system pioneered by Bentinck was not universally enforced until 1875, and it was difficult to attain any real crowd control.

In the absence of gate money the courses depended on selling franchises to publicans, bookmakers and local hoteliers, while the railway companies organised 'specials' to bring the newly mobile punter to the track.

As anyone who has travelled on a 'special' to a sporting fixture will confirm, the facility can be a mixed blessing, to the extent that in the mid to late nineteenth century local patrons stayed away from their traditional meetings: 'The Master of the Hounds is busy among the cubs, the Lord Lieutenant is shooting partridges four or five fields off, and the Duke has shut himself up at home,' ran one contemporary account – all to avoid spectators best described as unwelcome.

Of course, none of these attitudes prevailed at such meetings as Ascot, Goodwood or Epsom which had no need of commercial support from the proletariat, and certainly not at Newmarket, where the lower orders were positively discouraged.

Inevitably, trouble literally brewed, especially on the scruffier London tracks such as Harrow, Kingsbury, West Drayton, Croydon, Lillie Bridge, Enfield, Bromley and Streatham. It goes without saying that these suburban delights were sponsored by publicans and bookmakers; hooliganism on a scale

Below: The Arrival by James Pollard – by van. This was an expensive means of pre-rail transport invented by Lord George Bentinck. You can see the four post-horses being led away while the racehorses were unloaded. The driver's seat is swung away to allow them to get out.

THE STEAM AGE

The struggle to buy railway tickets at Epsom in 1847. Ascot for the smart but the Derby for the masses.

THE RAILWAY—FIRST CLASS.

SECOND CLASS.

THIRD CLASS.

only reflected at football grounds today was the natural consequence of race meetings essentially organised for the benefit of those taking bets or selling drinks.

Again the railways played a contributory role 'facilitating the movement of indolent roughs', and on the courses battles were engaged between welshing bookies and disgruntled punters while jockeys considered guilty of not trying had to dodge anything from ripped up iron railings to lynch mobs.

The Jockey Club had lost control and Parliament stepped in, requiring all courses within ten miles of Charing Cross to obtain a licence from local magistrates – a measure which eventually put the cowboy tracks out of business.

By now bad publicity had reduced racing in the perception of the nation's rulers, and in 1860 Lord Redesdale presented to the House of Lords a Light Weight Racing Bill. Redesdale's concerns were both humanitarian and in the interests of the breed. He argued that the ridiculously low weights allotted in some handicaps reflected on the

Left: Three levels of comfort getting to the races by train. Below: The advent of the railways revolutionised racing making courses accessible to horses trained all over the country.

ability of animals which should not be racing if so poorly evaluated and that 'child' jockeys were being exploited.

He asked for a minimum weight of 7st and settled for 5st 7lb after Lord Derby had presented a petition to the House suggesting that the organisation of the sport was best left to the Jockey Club.

The ruling body of any sport had to fight its corner against Parliamentary legislators, or slip into periods of ruinous impotence – as illustrated by the modern organisations who 'rule' some other sports. The disciplinary treatment of those who offend against the Rules of Racing may be even handed, some might say lax, by the harsh standards of the past; but it is fair to say that some of the prima donnas of the football field and the tennis court would not be tolerated for five minutes at Portman Square – and racing is the better for it.

Racing has always been under a searching Parliamentary eye, but luckily the sport has usually had its own legislators of the calibre of Bentinck, Rous, Bunbury, Rosebery and Hartington to protect it from excessive executive interference. It must be remembered that, but for Lord Hartington, the British Horseracing Board would not exist and the Turf would probably be under the thumb of a statutory British Racing Authority, acting under the will of Parliament.

At the end of his reign as 'Dictator of the Turf', Rous had headed off the rougher elements at both ends of the democratic scale. He had long since been promoted to Admiral on the reserve list, and for a quarter of a century his word was law in racing. Although he lacked the arrogance of Bentinck, he inevitably made some enemies – although these were well outnumbered by his friends, who arranged a testimonial dinner for him in 1865.

No person was allowed to contribute more than a 'pony' (£25) but four thousand pounds was collected. Henry Weigall was commissioned to paint the portrait which now hangs on the staircase at the Jockey Club in Newmarket, appropriately next to a likeness of Lord George Bentinck. In return Rous willed to the Club the priceless picture of Gimcrack by Stubbs which adorns the morning room at Newmarket and the painting of HMS *Pique* labouring under heavy seas, now in the dining room of the Jockey Club's London head-quarters in Portman Square.

The presentation, which included two candelabra with brass reliefs illus-trating Rous's exploits over the years, took place at Willis's Rooms in St James's Square in 1866. The dinner, described as 'a simple affair', encom-passed nine courses including such gastronomic delights as turtle soup, turbot, quail, lamb cutlets, forcemeat balls, mutton, York ham, venison, duckling and iced fruit pudding.

The Admiral also bequeathed the definitive handicap, the weight-for-age scale, which he drew up in 1850 and is still in use today – with only minor adjustments made by the late David Swannell, then Senior Handicapper, in 1976.

In manner, Rous was often brusque and the naval training which had served him so well in adversity was often evident in his quarter-deck language and general bearing. On the other hand he was a convivial companion, even if when crossed he resembled the bull in John Dryden's *Conquest of Granada*.

Monarch like, he ranged the tented field
And some he trampled down, and some he killed.

When the Admiral died in 1877, the Edwardian era was truly underway – notwithstanding that the period is usually intended to reflect the short reign of King Edward VII between January 1901 and May 1910. For racing it was a time of comparative calm; Rous had steered his last command safely into port, but when the voyage was resumed, his successors found rocks ahead and had to resist a particularly nasty and unsporting invasion force.

CHAPTER 6

Members and Guests

Before considering the Edwardian period in detail, it might be as well to review the membership of the Club during the period of Bentinck and Rous.

When strong personalities dominate any field of activity for a long time, it is easy to forget those whom you might call the supporting players. Churchill cast a huge shadow over his wartime coalition government, but he was aided by such men as Ernest Bevin, Lord Beaverbrook and Clement Attlee. Similarly, Attlee when Prime Minister looked to Bevin again, Nye Bevan and Harold Wilson, who in turn headed administrations which included Roy Jenkins and Barbara Castle.

Sir Joseph Hawley, born in 1814, had a considerable influence on the Turf in the middle of the nineteenth century. He could trace his family to pre-Norman times, and although his ancestor the Thane of Leybourne led his men against the Conqueror at Hastings, the Thane managed to escape the confiscation of his lands in Kent.

Notwithstanding an unsuccessful expedition to the Crusades in the company of Richard I, the Hawleys increased their wealth and Sir Joseph inherited a considerable fortune from his father, Sir Henry, including a large area of north London known as Kentish Town.

Declining to represent the quaintly if obviously named 'Shire of the Hops' in Parliament in the tradition of many of his forebears, Hawley served in the 9th Lancers for the customary brief period and then cruised the Mediterranean in his schooner *Mischief*. Morocco, Greece and Sicily all played hostess to the well-named *Mischief* before Hawley settled in Florence to immerse himself in a study of the fine arts and *belles lettres*. As a relief from this exercise of the cultured mind, Sir Joseph imported a few hairtrunks from England to compete against even less illustrious animals on the Florentine racetrack.

His partner in the venture was J M Stanley, and the two expatriates 'cleaned up'. Although he maintained his lifelong interest in art and literature, and established a superb library at his home, Leybourne Grange, in 1844 Hawley and Stanley registered their colours of 'Cherry and Black Cap', whence Hawley became absorbed in racing.

Perhaps it was his early experience of winning in circumstances which blatantly favoured him, or the quirk of nature which makes a bad loser, but when not behaving as a pillar of the Turf establishment, Sir Joseph Hawley's activities were often best described as 'warm'.

To the disgust of Rous he was over-indulgent to his jockeys, frequently giving the little men the whole stake after a rich victory. The over-generosity was perhaps symptomatic of Hawley's basic flaw and the Admiral and the aesthete nearly came to blows after the Doncaster Cup in 1851.

Sir Joseph Hawley the most successful – but unpopular – owner of the 19th century.

Under the Rules prevailing at the time, and specifically Rule 40, no person could enter or run two horses of which he was whole or part owner for any plate, even if entered in another person's name, i.e. a partnership.

Sir Joseph entered both The Ban and Vatican for the race on Town Moor and someone blundered at Weatherby's because both nominations were accepted. The Ban won the race, and naturally enough the owner of the runner-up objected. Sir Joseph swore that he had sold Vatican just before the race. The matter of Vatican's entry came before the Stewards of the Jockey Club and white smoke emanated from the chimney of the Committee Room.

Henry Chaplin, the Steward, was also the owner of Hermit in the infamous 1867 Derby when he defeated his arch rival Henry 4th Marquess of Hastings.

The Stewards allowed The Ban to keep the race, adding a rider to the effect that the Doncaster stewards should not have allowed Vatican to run.

It could be argued that they should not have allowed The Ban to run either, and black smoke belched from more than one stack as many turfites refused to believe that the 'sale' of Vatican had been genuine. So affronted was the gentle Sir Joseph that he announced his retirement from the Turf. Happily, this was of short duration, but a little while later Hawley was involved in an even greater scandal.

The financial indulgence towards his jockeys was not entirely philanthropic and the munificence had to be earned. In 1867 Hawley had some outstanding animals in training; Green Sleeve won the Middle Park from his stable companion Rosicrucian, winner of the Criterion Stakes, then a top juvenile contest; and Blue Gown, sired by Hawley's Derby winner Beadsman, was first past the post in the Champagne Stakes at Doncaster.

Sir Joseph's jockey was 'Tiny' Wells, who had won many good races for his patron, including the Two Thousand Guineas and the Derby in 1858 on Fitz-Roland and Beadsman respectively and the 1859 Derby on Musjid. However, following nearly a decade of successful and well-rewarded riding, the appellation 'Tiny' (real name John) no longer applied and the jockey was getting distinctly portly for one of his profession. This condition was not improved by sitting up all night drinking at the card table.

The upshot was that Wells had no chance of drawing the correct weight of 8st 10lbs on Blue Gown for the Champagne Stakes, although the usual 'toe on the floor' technique employed by all cheating jockeys enabled him to weigh out successfully. Unluckily for Wells the subterfuge was observed by his fellow riders, if not by the Clerk of the Scales, and when he returned to weigh in, two jockeys, Doyle and Watson, appealed to Henry Chaplin who was a steward of the meeting.

Chaplin ordered Wells to remain in the weighing chair until Admiral Rous could be summoned, together with Sir Joseph. Rous would not allow the usual two pounds given to jockeys in such circumstances to be placed on the scales, declared the unhappy Wells to be overweight and Blue Gown was disqualified.

Sir Joseph Hawley was not best pleased as can be imagined, but he had the compensation of knowing that Blue Gown had 'won' the Champagne Stakes carrying in excess of 9st, although the actual overweight was never made public. Clearly with at least 5–6lbs in hand a somewhat 'good thing' for the following year, Blue Gown duly won the 1868 Derby and Wells received the prize money of £6,000 from Hawley, who by now disliked Blue Gown so much that he sold the horse to Prussia for £5,000.

A proud man, Hawley became known as 'Dangerous Sir Joseph' and not entirely for his success on the Turf. He successfully sued Dr Shorthouse, founder of the *Sporting Times*, for libel. The unlucky doctor was committed to prison in default of damages and Hawley refused all the blandishments of his friends to intervene with the authorities and secure a remission of the sentence.

Dr Shorthouse consoled himself with his wine allowance of one quart of champagne *per diem* and when released in March 1870 found Hawley heavily engaged in Turf reform.

Sir Joseph's campaign was on three fronts. Firstly, he came out very strongly against the racing of two-year-olds; secondly he wished to expand the base of the Jockey Club; his third target, obvious but unspoken, was Rous.

Hawley was not the only one who considered that the breed had been weakened by juvenile racing which provided gambling owners with a quick return, as noted in Chapter Three. Rous, on the other hand, thought that the quality of the English thoroughbred was constantly improving, believing that the racing of two-year-olds was not an evil in itself, but that the owners abused the system by consistently over-racing young stock. The Admiral also expressed the extraordinary theory that the virtual abolition of juvenile racing at Newmarket, as he thought endemic in Hawley's proposals, would mean financial ruin for Headquarters since the Jockey Club had no power to impose the sanction on other courses which would cash in accordingly.

This ludicrous suggestion brought forth a broadside from *The Times*, the Admiral's favourite paper, commenting, 'If the day comes when the authority of the Jockey Club extends no further than The Ditch it will be because its members were not equal to their position, and had not the courage to exercise for the public good the powers which rest in their hands.' Going on to support Hawley, the editorial averred that racing had become a mere gambling business, resulting in 'the monstrous development of two-year-old racing'.

The next meeting of the Jockey Club was during Epsom week and the following resolutions sponsored by Sir Joseph were considered:

1. That no two-year-old shall run earlier in the year than 1st July.
2. That no two-year-old shall start for any handicap.
3. That in future no money shall be added from the funds of the Jockey Club to any race for which two-year-olds may be entered.
4. That if two or more two-year-olds run a dead-heat they shall not be allowed to run again, but the prize shall be equally divided between them.

Not surprisingly the meeting attracted an almost maximum attendance, if only because the aged and infirm would have missed the Derby, but the impressive turnout did not help Hawley's cause. Rous spoke vehemently against the proposals, although Lord Stradbroke, patronisingly referred to by the Admiral as 'my poor, foolish brother', was in favour. This was doubtless a symptom of filial disarray usually cloaked by the dubious theory of family unity.

At all events, the first proposal was defeated by 25 votes to 7; the second and fourth went down by 24 to 16 and Hawley withdew the third. Common humanity should have ensured at least the success of the fourth proposal, but as Roger Mortimer observed, the aristocratic sportsmen were used to having their own way and reserved the right to ruin their own horses if they wanted to do so.

There was an element of hypocrisy in Hawley's suggestions. He had won the Middle Park twice in the first three years of its existence, gambling successfully on each occasion for huge sums. Even as his ideas were being debated, he was landing a nice touch in a two-year-old race at Northampton and during the winter he had taken £40,000 to £600 each about his five juvenile fillies entered for the Derby.

These activities did not pass without comment, but undeterred Hawley returned to the fray. This time his target was the Club itself. Anticipating events by some 120 years, he proposed, among other matters, 'That in addition to the private meetings of the Jockey Club, there also be public meetings of that body at which alone motions to rescind, alter or add to the Laws of Racing shall be made', and, 'That the basis of the Club be extended, and that not only more gentlemen who are large owners of racehorses, but those who take an interest in racing as a means of preserving the breed of horses, be invited to become members'.

A suggestion which would find favour in some quarters today to the effect that, 'When a horse did not start, all bets should become void with the sanction of warning-off and disqualification from making entries be imposed on anyone paying out or receiving money from any bet so voided', was not adopted; but again Sir Joseph was ahead of his time.

The British Horseracing Board today owes its existence to the need to reform from within before being subjected to reform from without. Hawley's ideas for broadening the democratic base of the Club were sensible and practical enough by the standards of the time, but the Club led by Rous would not have it. The battle raged in the Press, many journals being in favour of reform with the ironical exception of the sporting papers, then as now heavily dependant upon the bookmakers and tipsters advertising support.

Rous hit back at *The Times* in a letter in which he underlined a weakness in the argument that racing was becoming a business, not a sport. The Admiral asserted that racing had always been a trade and a good one from 1858 to 1868, the principal span of Hawley's career, going on to say that one of his friends had won £75,000 on a single race and another friend, £115,000. This was a clear allusion to Hawley and Henry Chaplin, who supported Sir Joseph in his reforms.

As a cosmetic exercise, the Stewards set up a Reform Committee to consider the state of the sport. Apart from agreements to amend the start of the flat racing season from mid-February to the end of March and that there should be no two-year-old handicaps before 1st October, nothing had changed. Hawley retreated from the Turf a broken man and when 'Tiny' Wells died at the age of 39 in 1873, Sir Joseph broke up his stud. He died of rheumatic gout two years later.

Until the formation of the B.H.B. in June 1993 sporadic attempts to reform the Jockey Club all failed, but that is not to say that the Club remained static in social attitudes, administrative skills and responsibility to the punters and racegoers. Hawley was an intellectual with little time for those less intelligent than himself. Diplomacy was not his strong point and many found the bluff, straightforward old sea-dog Rous easier to understand. Sir Joseph was probably 'too clever by half' and it is often the fate of clever people to be misunderstood. Superior intellect can frighten the less cerebrally well-endowed, as many politicians have found to their cost.

Another thinker who enjoyed some stature on the Turf at the time was the diarist Charles Greville. A typically old-style Whig aristocrat and a congenital bachelor, he had little time for the proletariat, preferring the convivial social life of St James's clubs and the company of those involved at the highest level in politics and field sports.

Greville's discretion, independence of mind and sophisticated wisdom made him a natural referee in matters of personal, financial and matrimonial difficulty – and affairs of honour. He brought the same razor-sharp mind to his duties as a Steward of the Jockey Club, although a heavy and not very successful gambler.

Like Hawley, and indeed anyone who raced on a considerable scale even in partnerships or 'confederacys' as they were know at the time, Greville suffered some unfortunate moments. In 1842 his colt Canadian was a strong ante-post bet for the Derby. Not long before the race Canadian fell lame, as horses sometimes do. Greville naturally hedged his own bets before scratching Canadian, an action which infuriated the easily disgruntled punters who did not seem to have heard of the phrase 'caveat emptor'.

The *Sunday Times* also broke out in a rash of moral indignation, and Greville's request for an apology merely brought a second broadside in which he was accused of withdrawing Canadian only because he had laid heavily against the horse. In an action for libel, the jury awarded Greville £250 damages.

A few years later Lord Stanley's Cazenove started a 13/8 on favourite for the Goodwood Cup. Greville entered his horse Cariboo as a pace-maker for Cazenove and declared accordingly. However, Cariboo was a good horse in his own right and his jockey, Charlton, had to take a pull in the last two hundred yards in order to let Cazenove win.

Naturally, the bookmakers were rather cross, notably one William

'Leviathan' Davis who swore at Greville after the race. The bookmaker-sup-ported papers joined in, one printing the astonishingly witty headline which would have warmed the hearts of tabloid editors today: 'CARIBOO – BOO! – BOO!'

The elegant Greville laughed it off. He certainly did not benefit financial-ly, as he regarded odds-on favourites as a mug's bet strictly for the 'plebs'. Davis, who started the first betting lists in *The Strand,* later cleared £50,000 over the Autumn Double in 1853 when Hero won the Cesarewitch at 50/1 and Little Davis took the Cambridgeshire at 33/1. On this occasion, Davis's luck was in, as Parliament made betting houses illegal shortly afterwards.

Like many aesthetes, Greville found racing both fascinating and repug-nant at the same time. He was particularly disgusted by the habitués of the racecourse, an emotion which he might feel at some of the more 'popular' meetings today. He hated Epsom more than anywhere, and again there is a comparison in contemporary terms. He wrote in his diary before leaving to witness the Derby of 1838, 'Racing is just like dram drinking, momentary excitement and wretched intervals full consciousness of the mischievous effects of the habit and equal difficulty in abstaining from it.'

Later he added, 'These are my holidays, exclusively devoted to the Turf, passed in complete idleness, without ever looking into a book, or doing one useful or profitable thing, living with the merest wretches, whose sole and per-petual occupation it is jockeys, trainers, bettors, blacklegs, people who do nothing but gamble, smoke and talk everlastingly about horseracing.'

The aforementioned Lord Stanley, owner of Cazenove, was later the 14th Earl of Derby. A magnificent orator, he was three times Prime Minister and known as 'The Rupert of Debate', a reference to the 17th-century dashing cavalry general Prince Rupert of the Rhine.

Derby's racing career was comparatively brief, lasting only twenty-one years until politics and literature claimed him. One art form which did not captivate Derby was music. Every piano at his seat, Knowsley in Lancashire, had to be locked when he was in residence. His chief contribution to the Turf was to persuade the Jockey Club to warn-off owners and others who had been found guilty of cheating in other walks of life. Today such person are 'exclud-ed' which is very much the same thing.

Another distinguished politician who had little free time from two lengthy Premierships was Lord Palmerston who became the first Liberal MP in 1859, when in his seventies and having led the country to victory in the Crimean War.

An Irish peer with no automatic seat in the House of Lords, Palmerston was elected to the Commons and held ministerial office for forty-five years. Nonetheless, he indulged in racing as much as his comparatively modest means would allow and always had a few animals in training, mostly with the Day family at Stockbridge in Hampshire. His successes were in keeping with his pocket, but his prestige as a great leader and politician rubbed off on the

Jockey Club, although he took no part in racing administration.

Palmerston is best remembered as a turfite for the victory of his filly Iliona, who landed a gamble in the Cesarewitch. The horse had cost the future Prime Minister only sixty-five guineas, but her triumph in 1841 was a little over-shadowed by a fierce debate over how to pronounce her name.

It would seem a trifling matter to those of us who work as broadcasters nowadays and have to grapple with not only the mysteries of the Middle Eastern lexicon but also the gobbledygook produced by those who insist on calling their runners by an omnibus name reflecting the names of their moth-er-in-law, eldest daughter and the family cat, but the question was: should Iliona be pronounced with a short Ô or a long O? Many opted for the long version, but others, perhaps students of Homer, insisted on the short.

Like all good classical debates, and in this instance with the added spice of some hefty wagers on the outcome, the matter was referred to an impeccable academic source, none other than the Master of Trinity College, Cambridge. The Master came down on the side of 'the shorts'. What is not recorded is the way Palmerston himself referred to the filly. Perhaps he called her Illy?

A successful owner/Prime Minister, Lord Palmerston who won the Ascot Stakes with Buckthorn.

Two other prominent members of the Jockey Club at the time were General the Hon. George Anson and George Payne. Like Greville, Anson was a man of diplomacy and an expert adviser in matters of hon-our. When Squire Osbaldeston and Lord George Bentinck were unwisely drawn into a duel, it was Anson's handling of the affair, aided by the shrewd sup-port of George Payne, which averted a tragedy.

The General fought at Waterloo and as a colonel won the Derby with Attila in 1842 and the Oaks with The Princess in 1844. Doubtless he served the Jockey Club as well as he did his friends and it was a surprise to many when he accepted the command of a Division in India in 1853. Within three years, he was Commander-in-Chief. When the Mutiny erupted in 1857, Anson was giving a din-

No Turf history can be complete without this sketch of Rous and Payne.

ner party and naturally he did not embarrass his guests by opening the telegrams informing him of the situation whilst at the table.

This typically English display of good manners was unfortunate from the military point of view as the inevitable delay in the despatch of the C-in-C's orders was more helpful to the Sepoy mutineers than the British troops. A few days later, Anson took to the field himself, but he had not seen active service in forty-two years and died after the first day's march. His wine and beer supplies which he had laid in for the campaign were sold to the 9th Lancers' mess for £400. Clearly the General was wise enough to believe in the old military adage that you should never travel without your next bed or your next drink.

George Payne was well qualified to advise Bentinck and Osbaldeston on the dangers of duelling, as in 1810 his father was killed in a duel on Wimbledon Common. The other protagonist was a gentleman called Clarke, whose sister Payne senior had seduced.

Although the elder Payne had informed his second that he would not return Clarke's fire, the decision was academic as Clarke shot him in what was euphemistically called the groin, presumably in order to make the punishment fit the crime, irrespective of the rules and conventions of duelling.

Payne's reproductive organs were irreparably damaged and he died at four-thirty in the afternoon in the Tap Room of the Red Lion, Putney. The lady in the case and her brother were presumably unaware that sexual intercourse, short of rape, requires the co-operation of both parties.

However, such events were quite usual in Regency England, and the six-year-old Payne junior found himself the inheritor on coming of age of Sulby Abbey in Northamptonshire, £17,000 a year in rents and a fortune of £300,000 in 'ready money'. As the latter sum alone would be worth about a hundred million pounds today, George Payne was well insulated from the world.

His fondness for all forms of gambling did not allow him any time for Turf administration, but his great knowledge of betting made him much in demand as an arbitrator and he was an expert witness in the Law Courts. Not surprisingly Payne ran through three fortunes. He enjoyed little luck as an owner, his principal success being with Clementina in the 1,000 Guineas of 1847.

His chief contribution to the Turf was via his long friendship with Rous. There is little doubt that Rous derived much information not to say wisdom as the fruit of their association; wisdom well employed for the benefit of racing.

On his death, George Payne was described as a sterling English gentleman, the soul of honour, beloved by men and idolised by women, children and dogs. Who could ask for more?

CHAPTER 7

Deeds Fine and Foul

Prior to the death of Admiral Rous in 1877, three important measures were taken. The first, in 1843, was the decision to detach the Club as a ruling body from all matters connected with gambling. As previously noted this reform, necessary at the time to free the Club from an arbitrary role in betting disputes thus allowing the Stewards more time to adjudicate on purely racing affairs, was to be costly in the long term, but the Club could hardly have been expected to look over a century ahead.

The Rules under the heading 'Respecting Stakes, Forfeits and Bets' still stood in the *Calendar* but the Club issued a notice suggesting that 'all persons having disputes thereupon to decide the same by referees, one to be chosen by each of the parties and two to select a third'.

Secondly, there were several amendments to the Rules which were completely revised in 1858, replacing the set originally published in Mr Pond's *Kalendar* over a century before. The new code of sixty-five rules was intended to encompass the rapidly changing world of racing for the foreseeable future, but the expansion of the Turf made them obsolete just over a decade later.

So, in 1870, the Rules concerning horseracing in general were subject to a Jockey Club committee, as they had been in 1858, following which flat racing took on very much the shape that we know today, excluding all-weather tracks. The start of the season was defined as the week including 25th March, continuing to the week including 15th November. Restrictions were applied to two-year-old racing and the minimum distance for three-year-olds and upwards fixed at five furlongs.

It was the first time that 'flapping' tracks were defined as 'unrecognised meetings' as opposed to recognised meetings sanctioned by the Jockey Club, with the penalty of disqualification imposed on any owner, trainer, jockey or official taking part in an unrecognised meeting.

To reinforce these provisions, the Club extended the principle of licensing to include not only officials, trainers and jockeys but also racecourses, which had to comply with standards and conditions in accordance with the wishes of the Club.

Meanwhile, in 1866 the Club had abolished the clearly corrupt practice of judges accepting presents from winning owners. At the time, a judge was paid £50 by the owner of a Derby winner, £30 from whoever won the Oaks and the same amount in respect of the Cesarewitch and the Cambridgeshire. Extraordinarily, the Two Thousand Guineas was only worth a tenner, which if nothing else says something about the importance placed on handicaps in the mid-nineteenth century.

A further reform came in 1877 when a new regulation stated that all stakes should be paid to the winners by the Race Fund at Weatherby's within fifteen days of the race, and that any person in default for entries should be placed on the forfeit list and disqualified until the bill was paid.

This ensured prompt payment to the winner, who was relieved of the tiresome necessity of claiming the stakes from his defeated opponents, not an easy task allowing for human nature.

The third significant innovation had little enough to do with the Jockey Club or flat racing. It was the formation of the National Hunt Committee in 1866.

Famous racing Newmarket personalities 1885, Fred Archer up.

Mr Robert Peck		The Duchess of Manchester	The Prince of Wales	The Dowager Duchess of Montrose
Lord Hastings	Mat Dawson Captain Machell		The Duke of Portland	The Duke of Hamilton
Lord Rosebery	Mr Tattersall	The Marquis of Hartington		Mr Leopold de Rothschild
Mr Henry Chaplin	Earl Spencer Fred Archer		The Marquis of Londonderry	Sir John Astley
	Mr W.G. Craven			

The sport of steeplechasing had become established in the 1830s but, like the flat, fell into disrepute during the 'Filthy Forties' and 1850s; a situation not helped when horses were requisitioned by the government for the Crimean War.

There was no ruling body for chasing. The Jockey Club were not interested in a sport which they regarded as uncontrollable activities at worst and in the words of Admiral Rous 'an extraneous branch' of racing at best.

The prime mover towards the constitution of a ruling body was B J Angell,

St Albans.

STEEPLECHASING

Chasing, in spite of the opposition of Rous, eventually came under Jockey Club legislation – here are some races at Croydon, Kensington and St Albans – besides the Grand National (below) Dublin Flyer in the Cheltenham Gold Cup (bottom right).

Kensington.

Croydon.

well assisted by W G Craven. Benjamin Angell, better known as 'Cherry', owned Bridegroom, winner of the 1860 National Hunt Steeplechase at Market Harborough and the 1865 Grant National winner Alcibiade, at five years the youngest horse to win the world's most famous handicap chase. W G Craven was also a keen supporter of steeplechasing, but more importantly a member of the Jockey Club.

Angell, via the press, lobbied Admiral Rous with his own set of 'Rules and Regulations of the Steeplechase', which had been revised by 'many competent people' and had been 'shown to the principal racing and steeplechasing men of the day and been much approved of'.

'Cherry', an Old Etonian francophile who enjoyed both the intellectual and worldly delights of Parisian society, frequently restoring his liver at Baden-Baden, was never likely to receive more than a cool reception from the less sophisticated Rous. As put-downs go, it is a classic and well worth reading in full.

13 Berkeley Square
December, 1862

Although it is out of my jurisdiction as a Steward of the Jockey Club to interfere with the Rules and Regulations of the Steeplechase to be adopted at Market Harborough, I think it would be beneficial to the supporters of this extraneous branch of horseracing to suggest a few alterations which would tend to their efficiency and would assist the Steward in the event of the usual disputes.

The law-makers commence by stating that the rules concerning horseracing in general apply to all steeplechases. This is an error, because fourteen rules out of sixty-six have no application therewith. They omit Rule 42 which gives instructions to the starter. This is a very important article and, with a slight modification of fines, is essentially necessary to secure a fair start, otherwise there is no law to restrain a careless or unprincipled starter. Then, strange to say, Rule 43 is abolished, which forbids crossing and jostling, and prescribes a distance of two lengths or more before one horse can cross another's tracks, under the penalty of disqualification. Now if there is one rule in the racing code which is imperatively necessary for the existence of steeplechasing it is Rule 43. Nineteen disputes out of every twenty in steeplechasing originate from foul riding for which there are more inducements to indulge in than flat racing. A gap in a fence, a hard trodden path, a broken rail are all baits to seduce a rider to take unfair advantage, but by publicly ignoring the only rule to go straight the new code offers every encouragement to run riot and start unfairly. I am therefore at a loss to know how the Stewards are to decide disputes relative to starts and foul riding on their own responsibility when there is no law to ground a verdict of guilty in the event of one jockey riding over his neighbour, or of punishing the starter if he makes an unfair start.

Rule 2 has a more absurd termination 'there is no appeal whatever to a court of law'. This an imaginary edict, which would be laughed at even if it came from the Crown. No conventional agreement, no code drawn up by private individuals, can prevent a man in this country applying to a court of law for redress. Any person fancying himself aggrieved by the Stewards of races can and will appeal to a superior tribunal, although the printed racing programme states that 'the decision of the Steward is final', as I have discovered to my inconvenience.

All the other rules are well expressed and raising the standard weights to 12st 7lbs is a sensible improvement.

H. Rous

The reference to Market Harborough in the Admiral's letter concerns the National Hunt Steeplechase. The race was founded by Dr Fothergill 'Fogo' Rowlands in 1859. A leading amateur rider, principally in the blue and buff colours of the Earl of Strathmore which are now sported by the runners owned by HM Queen Elizabeth, the Queen Mother. When 'Fogo' retired from the saddle and took up training, one of his patrons was HRH the Prince of Wales.

The Prince did not register his colours until 1875. Born in 1841 he would have only just come of age in Royal terms when Market Harborough was the centre of the steeplechasing world. Socially the sport would have appealed to the Prince and the post-race entertainment was just up his street, led by the

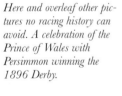

Here and overleaf other pictures no racing history can avoid. A celebration of the Prince of Wales with Persimmon winning the 1896 Derby.

Less often seen (right) – the shot of this very race being filmed with hand-cranked cameras.

delectable Caroline Walters, better known as 'Skittles' who was seen clearing the massive brook in her own fearless style.

'Skittles' earned the nickname from her original job setting up the pins in a skittle alley in the back streets of her native Liverpool, but her obvious attractions soon led her to become one of the most celebrated of the 'Bedroom Beauties'. She was the mistress of Lord Fitzwilliam, a Jockey Club member who, as Douglas Sutherland neatly observes in *The Yellow Earl*, allowed her 'unusual latitude in the matter of meeting his friends'. One of those was to be the Yellow Earl himself, the 5th Lord Lonsdale and a future Senior Steward.

Although a fine rider to hounds, 'Skittles' was socially ineligible to be received at any of the hunting house parties and therefore entertained her friends at the Haycock Hotel in Wansford, which remains an excellent hostelry to this day. The Prince certainly would have known her when she set up as a lady of the 'demi-monde' in London, driving through Hyde Park and riding in Rotten Row.

At all events, it was to National Hunt racing that the Prince turned when he first went into ownership via 'Fogo' Rowlands training establishment at Epsom. The Prince's lifelong friend, Lord Marcus Beresford, acted as his racing manager. Initially, Royal success was scanty and even his 1887 Sandown Military Gold Cup winner

Left: Skittles riding in the Bois de Boulogne. Quelle chic, quelle élégance, quelle grâce à cheval! Quite something for a girl from the slums of Liverpool after her dramatic liasion with Lord Hartington. She lived to eighty-one much loved and admired – even by the ladies of her day.

Hohenlinden was disqualified as his owner did not satisfy the conditions of the race, the Prince not being an officer of the army or navy on full or half pay.

Subsequently, the Prince was very successful under both Jockey Club and National Hunt rules, winning the Grand National with Ambush II in 1900, and eight classic races including three Derby winners and Triple Crown with Diamond Jubilee. There can be little doubt that the royal patronage of the winter game was as significant in the late nineteenth and early twentieth century as that bestowed by the Queen Mother today.

To return to 'Fogo' and his friends Angell and Craven, they did not give up easily. The National Hunt Committee had emerged in 1863, albeit self-elected, and was formally constituted in 1866 with the full agreement of the Jockey Club who were doubtless pleased to see the back of them. The Club emphasised the point in 1867 when resolving 'that in future Hurdle races shall not be considered as coming within the established Rules of Racing and shall not be reported in the *Calendar* with flat races'.

Thus left to their own devices, 'Cherry' and Co. applied themselves to the administration of the winter sport. Gradually the two branches of racing grew together, until the National Hunt Committee merged with the Jockey Club in 1969.

In 1866, when the Club politely told the National Hunt Committee to plough their own furrow, journalists were already reminiscing about the Newmarket of old and things being not what they were. John Corlett, Editor of the *Pink Un*, wrote:

Lord Marcus Beresford, one of the greatest gentleman riders of his day – both on the flat and over the sticks – was the Prince's racing manager.

> The picturesqueness of Newmarket is gone... We look in vain for the handsome figure of Lady Westmorland on horseback, the beautiful seat of Lady Astley and Madame Lévevre, the handsomest woman we ever saw at Newmarket... We miss Mrs Rous in her yellow chariot, with Lady Cardigan sitting by her, and we do not hear Mr George Payne telling Lord Glasgow, after one of his horses had unexpectedly upset Friponnier, that one of the 'legs' had taken 1,000 to 100 about him (and) the rosy-cheeked handsome Lady Mary Craven whose husband was the best-dressed man in London...

> The Heath remains much as it was, but profaned by many buildings. Reverence is no longer paid to the ditch and few salute it. Fewer still know what it was put there for. If to divide the Saxon kingdoms of East Anglia and Mercia, why not have Home Rule for these kingdoms and make the Stewards of the Jockey Club the Great Lords?

Lord Rosebery the fifth Earl wins the Derby (Ladas from the Mentmore Stud) and becomes Prime Minister in the same year 1894. The Prince of Wales looks on.

A fine compliment to the Club from Corlett, who clearly had a glad eye for the ladies as well, but in truth the Club had enough to do without ruling East Anglia, even if racing was losing most of its disreputable image; a process which accelerated as the final years of the nineteenth century approached.

The closing of many of the rougher London tracks as they were gradually replaced by the park courses were important moves, as were the stiffer licensing conditions, which insisted on a straight mile and proper provision for races over a distance of ground, with no dividend exceeding 10 per cent per annum paid to shareholders and accounts open to inspection by an appointee of the Jockey Club.

The patronage of the Prince of Wales smoothed the path and racing was not short of men with ability to play their part as members and Stewards of the Club. Lord Rosebery, who was elected to the Club in 1870, was Prime Minister when Ladas won the Derby in his rose and primrose colours in 1894.

The Club could lay claim to several of the principal statesmen of the day within their membership, and this gave the Jockey Club a power and prestige outside racing which would be unthinkable today. Another great political leader was the Marquess of Hartington, later the Duke of Devonshire; others included Lord Randolph Churchill (father of Sir Winston, himself a future member) and previously a Chancellor of the Exchequer, the Lords Londonderry and Zetland, both former Lords Lieutenant of Ireland, James Lowther, Secretary of State for Ireland, Lord Cadogan and Henry Chaplin, ex-cabinet ministers; the Duke of Richmond, Secretary for Scotland and two distinguished members of the judiciary, Sir Henry Hawkins and Lord Russell, Lord Chief Justice.

Land and mammon were represented by Lord Falmouth and the Dukes of Westminster and Portland. They won thirty-eight classics between them, but perhaps the greatest character of the period was Sir John Astley, popularly known as 'The Mate'. Far from enjoying vast wealth Astley was a poor man and had to depend on his gambling skills to finance his high standard of living and maintain a string of race horses.

Astley served as Tory MP for North Lincolnshire for a few years, but was far too outspoken and honest to succeed as a politician. Devoting his energies

to the Turf, he became a Steward in 1875, and in 1876 was chairman of the committee which framed the new Rules of Racing. He was responsible for building a new stand at the top of the Rowley Mile, but his greatest concern was for what we now call Racing Welfare. To his memory the Astley Club which he founded as a recreational institute for the hard-working stable lads serves that purpose to this day.

Different again from Sir John was the elegant Earl of Durham, elder brother of the Hon. George Lambton whose training skills spanned the late Victorian and Edwardian eras, plus two world wars.

George Lambton will reappear later in this chapter, but in 1887, as Queen Victoria celebrated her Golden Jubilee, it was Durham who held centre stage on the Turf. The Earl had served as a Steward of the Club although he was still in his thirties and suffered a great personal sorrow when his wife became mentally ill a few weeks after their marriage in 1882. The illness was found to be incurable.

Sir John Astley, 'The Mate' who came from a poor family but ended a very successful owner known for his loyalty to his chosen jockeys George Fordham and Charlie Wood. Weighing over 16 stone he took on (and beat) another Jockey Club member (Caledon Alexander) of the same weight in a match at Newmarket in 1879. Here he is on Drumhead, the horse he won it on.

A fellow Steward was Sir George Chetwynd, who enjoyed the benefit of being educated firstly at Eton and then at Harrow, playing against his former school at Lords in 1867. In the light of subsequent events some regarded this pluralism as an early sign of a duplicitous nature.

Sir George, like 'The Mate', lacked the means to sustain an extravagant way of life and depended on gambling for his income and the ability to repay the egregious Cork Street money-lender Sam Lewis for funds injected when results were adverse.

However, they were not always as adverse as they might or even should have been. Sir George maintained a large string at Chetwynd House in Newmarket. The stables had been purpose-built by Sir George's jockey Charlie Wood, adjacent to a cottage which Wood had purchased from Sir John Astley, and named in honour of his patron.

It transpired that Wood was rather more than a mere employee. In fact, he owned the majority of the equine inmates of Chetwynd House and although he transferred the ownership of the horses to Sir George in 1883, when the Jockey Club forbade professional

riders to own racehorses, it was no more than a paper transaction.

Sir George's trainer, Richard 'Buck' Sherrard, was a fine stableman but no great judge of form and certainly not able to place animals to win on a scale commensurate with Chetwynd's gambling. On the other hand Wood was a past-master at the art and had the advantage of being able to ride the horses with all the skills of a champion jockey; he headed the list in 1887 with 151 winners.

Wood might have improved on that had he not blatantly stopped many of his mounts to suit Sir George's betting book, actions which attracted the attention of no less an august publication than the *Licensed Victuallers Gazette*, whose racing correspondent wrote: 'How about the running of Success at Lewes and at Alexandra Park, where Charley Wood nearly pulled his head off on each occasion!'

Ironically, the outcome was rather like Ian Fleming's famous fictitious golf match between James Bond and the villain Goldfinger, where the latter unquestionably cheats all the way round, but not on the 18th green where Bond claims, and gets, the spoils. Almost everyone agreed that Wood had tried for his life on Success in both races. He brought a libel action against the *Licensed Victuor* but the jury were unconvinced and awarded the jockey a contemptuous farthing in damages.

It so happened that Lord Durham was due to make a speech at the annual dinner of the Gimcrack Club in York. Since the formation of the club in 1767 in honour of the pony-sized grey who won twenty-six races without troubling the judge at York, a tradition had formed which required the speakers to discourse on serious matters of the Turf. Durham needed no better excuse to make reference to the inconsistent running of horses sent out by a well-known Newmarket yard. He was clearly referring to Chetwynd House and although there was no mention of the name in his speech, he did not trouble to deny subsequently that it was Sherrard's stable that he had in mind.

Chetwynd was in a difficult position. His initial reaction was to challenge Durham to a duel, but

Marquess of Hartington and Lord Westmoreland both distinguished members of the Jockey Club. Although a prominent owner Hartington did not always recognise his own horses due to his preoccupation with Parliamentary debates on agriculture.

Lord Falmouth who hardly ever bet on his brilliantly successful horses in the 1870s.

apart from the fact that this now illegal pastime was also rather unfashionable, it would not clear the question of his honour even if he shot the Earl dead.

Good old-style compromise prevailed. Both Durham and Chetwynd agreed that the elaborate technicalities of racing required analysis by those familiar with the sport and not a judge chosen at random whose knowledge of the Turf might be limited to his local hunt fixture. Eventually, the Right Hon. James Lowther, the Earl of March and Prince Soltykoff agreed to adjudicate. All were Jockey Club members.

George Chetwynd.

The case was convened in 1889 and Lord Durham made two principal accusations: firstly, that Chetwynd employed Wood to prevent horses from showing their form until it was convenient for betting purposes to do so and that Wood enlisted the assistance of other jockeys in the race when his mount was 'off', for financial reward; secondly, that these and other malpractices were conducted with Chetwynd's connivance, thus encouraging Wood to break the Rules of Racing.

Sir George claimed £20,000 damages from Lord Durham and he proved to be a competent witness, cool under pressure. When Durham's specific accusation that Wood had stopped a horse called Fullerton with Sir George's full knowledge was not proven, it seemed that Chetwynd might yet be vindicated, but his evidence showed that he clearly lived by betting and had not paid Wood's annual retainer of £300 for several years. In short, he was no more than a professional punter, and a crooked one at that.

'Buck' Sherrard and Wood were fiercely cross-examined by Charles Matthews QC and Sir Charles Russell, both acting for Lord Durham. Sherrard fell apart completely and admitted total ignorance of the goings-on in his name. Wood was a tougher nut to crack, but it soon became obvious that the jockey had been assisted by Chetwynd to disregard the Rules of Racing which Sir George as a member of the Jockey Club was honour bound to obey.

The adjudicators awarded Chetwynd a farthing damages. He at once resigned from the Jockey Club, eventually retiring to Monte Carlo where he died in 1917. Wood was warned off, but his licence was restored in 1897. Typically, Lord Durham gave Wood his first mount on his return and he went on to enjoy a fruitful second career, including the Triple Crown on Galtee More and riding ten classic winners in all. Sherrard was no longer allowed to train in Newmarket, but was free to continue elsewhere. He resumed at Royston, not a million miles from HQ and won the Ascot Stakes with Scullion in 1902.

Important as it was in the context of the integrity of the sport, the Chetwynd affair paled in comparison to the events of 1903, when the very basis of racing was found to be in dire peril.

Tod Sloan, a much better export from the US at the turn of the century, who did much to change the traditional upright long leather style of race riding in this country. Unfortunately he too fell for the temptations of the less savoury side of racing and in 1900 was told by the Jockey Club not to bother to apply for a licence (see p. 74).

The poison striking at the roots of the Turf literally came from America. John Huggins, the walrus-moustached American who trained at Heath House, Newmarket, at the turn of the century, and won the Derby with Volodyovski in 1901, was once asked if there were many crooks on the American Turf. 'No,' Huggins replied, 'they have all come over here to England.'

One or two American owners had succeeded in Britain during the second half of the nineteenth century, notably Richard ten Broek whose American-bred stayers won the Cesarewitch, the Goodwood Stakes, the Ascot Stakes and the Goodwood Cup and Pierre Lorrilard, owner of Iroquois, the Derby and St Leger winner of 1881. James Keene's Foxhall was not entered in the classics, but considered by many to be superior to Iroquois and indeed won the Cesarewitch, the Cambridgeshire, the Grand Prix de Paris and the Ascot Gold Cup.

Those American owners were the straight guys; the Paul Mellons and William Woodwards of their time. Unfortunately, there were plenty of gentlemen of lesser scruples involved in American racing and by the late nineties the essentially puritan soul of the average US citizen had rebelled against the villainy being perpetrated under their noses. A strong anti-racing lobby grew and accordingly owners, trainers and jockeys, horses and a good number of unsavoury hangers-on crossed the 'herring pond' to try their luck in Britain.

We all know that luck is a lady, and like all ladies she likes to be flattered and encouraged from time to time. The Americans had a unique way of assisting the lady in question by artificial stimulants, or dope.

The methods and the drugs employed were crude in type and dosage by comparison with the sophisticated designer drugs and masking agents of today, although cocaine was administered along with horrors such as arsenic.

To be fair to the Americans, the practice was encouraged by their system of racing. Meetings would last for anything up to a month and then the circus would move on to another venue. Animals were raced on artificial surfaces to provide eight-, ten- or even twelve-race cards. 'Coke' in particular geed-up the jaded equine and also concealed the pain in the limbs of jarred-up runners.

Medication still haunts American racing today as students of the Breeders' Cup will know. But in Europe it was just as unwelcome a hundred years ago as it is now, and rightly so. Nonetheless, doping in Britain by American trainers soon became an open scandal, but there was nothing in the Rules of Racing to prevent it.

The modus operandi was simple. A moderate horse would be purchased out of a selling race or at a dispersal sale. The animal would be at least a four-year-old with what little form it could boast fully exposed. Suitably stimulated, the horse would run in a race well above its class and be backed without fear of defeat. The plan was usually successful and it is estimated that the principal American dopers relieved the bookmakers of £2,000,000 between 1897 and 1901. In modern terms, we are speaking of £88,000,000.

A typical example was a horse called Royal Flush, a six-year-old trained by an obscure handler named Steel. Royal Flush seemed well past his best when he came up for sale but Enoch Wishard, who trained at Newmarket for his American compatriot James Duke, paid 450 guineas for him. Well 'hotted', Royal Flush duly won the Royal Hunt Cup in 1900 under 7st, and another jab with the hypodermic secured the Stewards Cup carrying 7st 13lbs two months later.

In 1903, a heavily doped horse won a race but the jockey was unable to pull up on the crazed creature. He bailed out and the animal crashed into a wall and died. The Hon. George Lambton, by now training for Lord Derby, attempted to bring matters to the attention of a steward of the Jockey Club, not only on the grounds that doping was playing havoc with the form and endangering lives human and equine, but also drawing attention to the serious menace that doping presented to breeding, a question which still rages over the American Turf today. Unsound or weak thoroughbreds insulated from the pain of infirmity or internal bleeding, may produce equally unsound stock.

Hon. George Lambton, fifth son of the second Earl of Durham, and his stable lads. Lambton maintained he was better at training jockeys than horses though after a brilliant show as an amateur rider he not only successfuly trained for the Earl of Derby but had much to do with setting up the Aga Khan's racing empire.

Lambton's plea fell on deaf ears. Accordingly, he decided to demonstrate the evil in the most practical fashion by running useless horses of his own under the influence of dope. He told his brother Lord Durham of his intention. The Earl was not happy but consented to the experiment provided that Lambton did not back the horses concerned.

Lambton obtained six dopes in small bottles from a veterinary surgeon. He used five of them on what he described as 'some of the biggest rogues in training', and four horses won, the other being second. None had shown a scrap of form before, and one animal called Ruy Lopez who had hitherto failed for the best jockeys in England, streaked up in the Lincoln Autumn Handicap, apprentice ridden.

Durham made sure that the message got through and shortly afterwards the Jockey Club passed the following Rule:

> If any person shall administer, or cause to be administered, for the purpose of affecting the speed of a horse, drugs or stimulants internally, by hypodermic or any other method, he should be warned off the Turf.

The rule was a 'sharp medicine' in the words of Sir Walter Raleigh, but unhappily it did not prove to be 'a sure cure for all ills'. With the benefit of hindsight, it was likely to be the cause of much injustice, as we shall see in later chapters, but it was right for its time and no legislation can be more than that.

The Americans sloped off to France to seek fresh fields to foul with their malodorous trade. Wishard, Duke, the barbed-wire magnate 'Betch-a-million' Gates and their discredited and warned-off jockeys all decamped leaving the British Turf a cleaner and better place. The irony was that Wishard was actually an excellent trainer, Tod Sloan was a brilliant jockey who revolutionised English race riding, and the brothers Lester and Johnny Reiff were nearly as good.

Sloan could not resist gambling and despite the patronage of Lord William Beresford and Lady de Bathe, formerly Lily Langtry, he was warned off for betting on his own ride Codoman in the 1900 Cambridgeshire. Lester Reiff won the Derby on Volodyovski in 1901 and was champion jockey the year before, but he came to grief after stopping De Lacey in the New Barnes Plate at Manchester, thus allowing his brother Johnny to win on Minnie Dee. Reiff never rode again.

Johnny Reiff was Enoch Wishard's first

Lily Langtry, the actress, who patronised Tod Sloan, was first mistress to the Prince of Wales and then that of 'the Squire', George Baird. Her relationship to Baird who lost over £2m on the racing game, like the story of the Yellow Earl, epitomised the era of Edwardian racing.

Police presence helped the Jockey Club clean up the racetracks. Below right: Enoch Wishard the American trainer who perfected the art of doping.

jockey and partnered the infamous Royal Flush. Dressed like a child in knickerbockers, he was the darling of some society ladies who frequently kissed him in the paddock, but the innocent countenance cloaked a cheating brain and Reiff had no compunction about stopping horses for the American gamblers who employed him.

He was not warned off but decided that the French air would be good for his health, returning to England for the occasional big race, winning the Two Thousand Guineas on Louvois in 1913 and the Derby on Orby in 1907 and Tagalie in 1912. He was first past the post at Epsom in 1913 on Craganour, only to be disqualified in favour of Aboyeur.

If the Jockey Club and the sport in general thought that they could heave a sigh of relief at the retreat of the American invaders, it was of short duration. Further American inspired trouble was brewing, this time on the equine rather than the human front.

CHAPTER 8

From Jersey to Sarajevo

By 1908, the anti-racing lobby in the United States, or more probably the anti-gambling lobby, seemed likely to secure legislation which would make betting on horseracing illegal. The measures proposed and endorsed by no less a figure than Governor Hughes of New York would have brought about a mayhem similar to the free-for-all induced by the prohibition of alcohol during the 'Roaring Twenties'.

American owners and breeders knew that once the gangsters moved in with illegal bookmaking, racing would be finished in any proper sense. They cast covetous eyes at Britain's well-run sport, basking in the sunset of the amiable Edwardian era.

Following the riding and training scandals which had marred the turn of the century, the Jockey Club rightly clamped down on the indiscriminate issuing of licenses, although some American trainers were warmly welcomed, such as Andrew Jackson Joyner who trained for H P Whitney and registered 480 winners in six years. Danny Maher, who was champion jockey in 1908, continued his fine career and achieved a popularity for a British-based American rider only equalled by Steve Cauthen more than seventy years later, but it is fair to say that American-bred horses were not so enthusiastically received.

The problem was not new. American pedigrees could not always be traced back so far as to show that they originated with British-bred stock. It followed that if British breeders used the services of American-breeds there was no certainty that the purity of the blood lines would be continued.

In 1901, the Jockey Club decided that only if eight or nine crosses of pure blood could be proved tracing back a hundred years or more, and if the racing performances of the animal's immediate family stood as evidence of the standard of the strain, then the horse could be entered in the General Stud Book.

This measure, although limiting to a great degree, let in a few imported horses and their offspring, but did little to pacify British breeders who were

rightly afraid of American-bred horses flooding the UK as racing in the United States collapsed. Accordingly, the amendment was rescinded in 1909, but was not retrospective as to those animals and their descendants admitted to the Stud Book in the previous eight years.

Further, more positive action was demanded by the breeding industry. The 8th Earl of Jersey had been elected to the Jockey Club in 1907 under his

courtesy title of Viscount Villiers. Three years later he was appointed a Steward and subsequently served as Senior Steward. His strong personality and natural administrative style, in which he combined a conservative instinct with an innovative mind, made his services invaluable to the Club; services which were tragically denied them by his death in 1923 at the age of forty-nine.

Jersey decided to take up the breeders' cause, and in the spring of 1913 put the following proposition to a meeting of the Jockey Club.

Whether, in view of the fact that a new volume of the Stud Book will be published this year, they (the Stewards) will consider the advisability of suggesting to Messrs Weatherby, the Editors, that the last sentence of the first paragraph of the preface be added to, so as to read as follows: 'They have decided in the interests of the English Stud Book no horse or mare can, after this date, be considered as eligible for admission, unless it can be traced, without flaw on both sire's and the dam's side of its pedigree, to horses and mares already accepted in earlier volumes of the book'?

The suggestion was adopted, and so what became known as 'The Jersey Act' was passed, and remained in force until 1949. The situation had become ridiculous in 1948 when neither My Babu, winner of the Two Thousand Guineas, or the St Leger winner Black Tarquin were eligible for the General Stud Book. The 'Act' was repealed, which was just as well since four of the next fifteen Derby winners, Galcador, Never Say Die, Larkspur and Relko would have been labelled half-breeds if the position as in 1901 had not be restored.

As it was, some good horses emerged during the period 1901 to 1908. Among the animals to be admitted then were Rhoda B, American Girl and Sibola. Rhoda B was the dam of 1907 Derby winner Orby, who in turn sired Grand Parade, winner of the premier classic in 1919. Descendants of American Girl included Mumtaz Mahal, Mahmoud, Nasrullah, Never Say Die, Tudor Minstrel and Palestine, while Sibola was the grand-dam of Nearco, sire of Dante and Nimbus.

On the other hand, horses forced into the half-breed list included the 1914 Derby winner Durban II. His descendants, amongst others were Djebel (Two Thousand Guineas) and Gold Cup winners Caracalla II and Arbar; all were ineligible for the Stud Book although winners of what are now Group 1 races.

It goes without saying the provisions of the Jersey Act went down like a dose of cold Boston tea in America. Nelson Dunstan, a leading American racing correspondent of the period, defined the attitude of his compatriots as follows:

There is small cause for surprise at the bitterness in America at the passage of the Jersey Act. By a single paragraph, England placed the stamp of 'half-bred' on American horses and, too, after our breeders had spent large sums of money on the importation of English horses. It was entirely natural that instances which bordered on the ridiculous would come to light. However, the stigma of 'half-bred' had a full effect on the markets of the world and as a consequence the export of sires and dams from the United States has shrunk to such proportions that it has become negligible.

The eighth Earl of Jersey, who was elected Jockey Club member in 1907, becoming Senior Steward in 1909 and again in 1923, the year he died.

His name is perpetuated on the turf through the "Jersey Act" which restricted admission to the General Stud Book for 36 years up to 1949. He was the great-grandson of the fifth Earl who was one of the most prominent owners and breeders of the first half of the nineteenth century, owning eleven classic winners including Bay Middleton and two other Derby winners.

The Act was unquestionably protectionism of the standard of which Lord George Bentinck and Disraeli would have been proud. Roger Mortimer, commenting in his master work *The Jockey Club*, penned as fine a piece of social observation as one can find, and it is well worth quoting in its entirety here:

It is a characteristic of members of the English race to be ignorant of the intense dislike they not infrequently inspire among persons of another nationality, and even if at length they become aware of this dislike, they tend to ignore it or at all events not to reciprocate it. It is one of the most annoying of Anglo-Saxon attitudes, and the searing Anglophobia, which is a common feature of a certain type of Irishman, is fanned to an even hotter pitch by the average Englishman's refusal either to return the hatred or to be in the slightest degree upset by it. He is too self-satisfied to imagine that the dislike could possibly be based on valid grounds.

However, Lord Jersey and the Club clearly acted with the best of intentions and were right to beware of unlimited immigration of sometimes suspect stock from a country bankrupt in racing terms. As it transpired, 1913 was to be a momentous year and a turning point not only for racing's little puddle, but for the civilised world.

DAILY SKETCH.

No. 1,323—THURSDAY, JUNE 5, 1913.   London: 46-47, Shoe-lane, E.C.   Manchester: Withy-grove   (Registered as a Newspaper)   ONE HALFPENNY.
Telephones—Editorial and Publishing, 6078 Holborn.   Advertisements 12,787 Central.

HISTORY'S MOST WONDERFUL DERBY: FIRST HORSE DISQUALIFIED: A 100 TO I CHANCE WINS: SUFFRAGETTE NEARLY KILLED BY THE KING'S COLT.

Miss Emily Davison.   The woman falling to the ground.   The King's horse, Anmer, falls on his jockey.   Herbert Jones.

Yesterday's Derby was extraordinary. Not only was Craganour, the favourite, disqualified after finishing first, the race being awarded to Aboyeur; a suffragette ran across the course at Tattenham Corner and seized the bridle of the King's horse. The King's horse and jockey were thrown to the ground, while the woman was nearly killed. The extraordinary photograph above was taken by the Daily Sketch a second after the horse and the woman fell to the ground.

The death of the suffragette Emily Davison under the heels of King George V's Anmer in the Derby was symptomatic. Whether Miss Davison was making a political gesture of protest which cost her her life, or she was simply crossing the track to use her return ticket to London from Tattenham Corner station and failed to see the tail-enders on the concave bend, we shall never know. But it is certain that the long Edwardian garden party of hot summers and bloated Christmases was over and a harshness was returning to the land; both political and military.

All seemed normal the following year. Once more the summer hummed its humid way, and events in minor Balkan states must have had little impact on a nation swimming, boating, sailing, thwacking the leather with the willow, the rubber with the catgut and looking forward to honey for tea.

It was a fool's paradise. In Sarajevo on 28th June 1914, Archduke Francis-Ferdinand of Austria-Hungary and heir to the throne was assassinated by a Bosnian student, Gaurico Princep, working for Serbian terrorists bent on a united South Slav State.

The Archduke had elected to visit the Bosnian capital on St Vitus' Day, the Serbian national festival. It was as advisable as King George V visiting Dublin on St Patrick's Day at the height of the Irish rebellion. Princep shot Francis-Ferdinand and his wife, a daughter of Queen Victoria, as they left a luncheon to visit an officer wounded in a bomb attack on the royal party earlier in the day.

Princep's shots ricocheted round

Emily Davison the Suffragette and the 1913 Derby.

A cheeky favour seeker catches up with George V and the royal party en route to Epsom.

Europe. Germany was committed to the repression of the Serbs on behalf of Austria-Hungary and secretly decided to go to war, but a 'phoney' period ensued. By mid-July English newspaper readers were engrossed in the trial of a former French Prime Minister's wife accused of shooting an editor who had threatened to publish her husband's letters to his mistress.

However, on 23rd July, Austria delivered an ultimatum to Serbia making demands which they knew to be unacceptable. War was declared on 28th July between Austria and Serbia. Russia then mobilised, intending to defend Serbia. On 1st August, Germany declared war against Russia, and two days later were at war with France as well.

Even so, the British Prime Minister, Herbert Asquith saw little reason for this country to be involved. Foreign Secretary, Sir Edward Grey thought differently. 'The lights are going out all over Europe,' he remarked sadly, knowing that any invasion of France by Germany through neutral Belgium would have to be resisted under the terms of the Treaty of Frankfurt signed at the end of the Franco-Prussian Wars in 1871.

Jockey Club members knew how to dress before the war. Left J. Holdsmith, right Sir Blundell Maple, M.P. and below the fabulous Yellow Earl, Senior Steward of the Club, with his long suffering wife, Grace.

In the words of a former leading stateswoman on the contemporary international stage, it was a 'Treaty too far', and expensive for Britain in more than a material sense; ten million lives were lost in the next four years.

But in August 1914 the sun still had his hat on and the people believed 'it would be all over by Christmas'. The false optimism soon evaporated and, by March 1915, the Turf authorities had to face up to the likely prohibition of horseracing. The proposition had been the subject of lively correspondence in *The Times* and at least three members of the Club had taken the view that racing should be suspended for the duration of hostilities. One of their number, the Duke of Portland, had been unduly influenced by a spurious story claiming that wounded soldiers were to be evacuated from the grandstand at Epsom in order that the Derby could be run as usual.

Lord Durham, the principal Jockey Club member at the time, supported by Lord Rosebery, a former Prime Minister, persuaded a meeting of the Club to continue to support a previous decision which stated racing should continue when conditions permit and 'the feeling of the locality is not averse to the meeting being held'. Durham himself never went racing during the war.

By 1917, the matter was again to the fore, this time at the insistence of an institution far more influential than even *The Times* namely, Parliament. David Lloyd George had become Prime Minister and his Government, with a classically unthinking libertarian conscience which would have made Mr Tony Benn green with envy, came to the conclusion 'that it was against public opinion that racing should be continued'.

Admittedly, racing had only continued on a 'dot and carry' basis mostly at Newmarket, where the 10,000 population were almost entirely dependant on the sport, and at Newbury with thirty racing stables quartered nearby. It wasn't really enough and the racing community protested strongly. Race companies were in financial straits, as no money was coming in, but they still had to maintain the courses and, for some extraordinary reason, contribute to the prize money at Newmarket. Even Epsom was reduced to selling the contents of the wine cellar to make ends meet.

However, a small breeding industry was maintained and the major races preserved. The classics were run at Newmarket, with the exception of the St Leger as the proud burghers of Doncaster refused to allow the race to be run anywhere but on Town Moor, which was impractical in wartime conditions. Rightly rejecting this parochial and somewhat dog-in-a-manger point of view, the Stewards authorised a 'September Stakes' run over one-and-three-quarter miles at Newmarket and recognised as the third leg of the Triple Crown, won

The Doncaster Race Committee. With stalwart men like these how could Doncaster have earned such a tarnished reputation? These proud burghers and their descendants objected to the St. Leger being run anywhere other than Town Moor even during the War.

in these circumstances by Pommern in 1915, Hurry On in 1916, Gay Crusader in 1917 and Gainsborough the following year.

Other arrangements included a June Stakes at Newmarket and with the blessing of Epsom a substitute Coronation Cup. A Newmarket Gold Cup replaced the Ascot centrepiece with £1,000 added by the Ascot Authority, a Stewards' Handicap was run at Newmarket with identical conditions to the Goodwood Stewards' Cup and a five furlong New Coventry Stakes, again with £1,000 contributed to the stakes by Ascot. In 1916, a substitute Lincolnshire Handicap was run at Lingfield under the ingenious if slightly obvious name of the Lincolnfield Handicap, while the Grand National moved to Gatwick in 1916 and stayed for a year, a sensation not unknown to air travellers today.

In 1916 the Jockey Club persuaded the Government to sanction additional meetings at Gatwick, Lingfield, Newbury and Windsor – all well away from centres of high population and munitions factories, the latter consideration not only a matter of literally explosive danger, but also potential absenteeism.

Northern trainers were obviously less than pleased, but they lost little since the Government soon rescinded the concession as a petrol shortage loomed. Racing was again confined to Headquarters, but the 1917 request to cease racing altogether came as a bolt from the blue. It must be emphasised that it was only a request, not an instruction, but nevertheless the Stewards complied, and cancelled all fixtures after the Spring Meeting in May, reasoning that compliance with a request from the War Cabinet would leave the door open for a resumption in time, whereas legislation might be difficult to repeal.

This time the breeders felt most aggrieved as the limitations on racing had already depressed the yearling market to 60 per cent, and what was effectively abolition would ruin the industry. Accordingly, Lord D'Abernon formed the

Thoroughbred Breeders Association to put their case to the Stewards. D'Abernon combined the talents of a fine military mind, financial expertise and scholarship which enabled him to compile a Modern Greek Grammar which became a standard work in Greece. A leading owner-breeder, he won the One Thousand Guineas with Diadem in 1917, and was years ahead of his time over misuse of the whip; Diadem was never touched with this equestrian aid.

The TBA flourishes to this day from its Headquarters at Stanstead House in Newmarket, but Lord D'Abernon and his fellow breeders need not have exercised themselves unduly. Lord Jersey, Senior Steward once more, Lord Rosebery and the Lords Durham and Crewe ably supported by the Quarter-Master General, the Director of Remounts the politician Lord Curzon, well backed by the racehorse owner and polemic journalist Horatio Bottomley, managed to persuade the Government to sanction forty days racing, as from 4th July 1917, in view of the 'national importance of horse-breeding'.

Following the Armistice of November 1918, racing resumed at full power a few weeks later. A boom ensued as demobilised servicemen flocked to the tracks with gratuities to spend. There were the inevitable strikes by the mining and transport workers, then and until recently the bulwark of left-wing political clout which eventually and literally undermined the fragile post-war economy, but until 1921, the racecourses were packed and 'eat, drink and be merry' was the order of the day.

Lord Durham maintained his dominance in the Jockey Club hierarchy and could safely be said to be the Bentinck of his time. He was a member from 1882 until he died in 1928 and was a Steward for five terms of office. He always acted with the greatest integrity and in the best interests of the Club, as instanced in the Chetwynd case. Even in the minor matter of smoking in the weighing room which he not only rightly prohibited but also rigorously enforced, he did not fear the inevitable unpopularity, being concerned only that non-smokers in a community of supposedly healthy athletes did not suffer.

It was one of Durham's achievements to have introduced that mixed blessing of former years, the starting gate. Tried out in 1898, the barrier became mandatory for two-year-old races in 1900 and went into general use in 1901, but it did not always perform satisfactorily and many preferred the old 'Bentinck' flag start; some still do.

ANNOUNCING THE START FROM TOP OF GRAND STAND

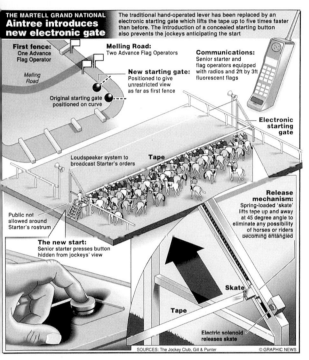

THE START

Several pictures showing starting since the camera was invented.

1 and 2: the stalwart, Arthur Coventry mounted and on foot (at Sandown); 3 and 4: the starting gate showing a few problems at Kempton; 5: the stalls'handlers at Newmarket; 6: a false start at Sandown; 7: the high tech tapes at Aintree and finally 8: the popular Captain Keith Brown being fêted on his retirement the year after the Grand National starting debacle.

The drawing opposite shows the start being announced in the grandstand at Goodwood.

THE MARTELL GRAND NATIONAL
Aintree introduces new electronic gate

The traditional hand-operated lever has been replaced by an electronic starting gate which lifts the tape up to five times faster than before. The introduction of a concealed starting button also prevents the jockeys anticipating the start

First fence: One Advance Flag Operator

Melling Road

Melling Road: Two Advance Flag Operators

New starting gate: Positioned to give unrestricted view as far as first fence

Original starting gate positioned on curve

Communications: Senior starter and flag operators equipped with radios and 2ft by 3ft fluorescent flags

Electronic starting gate

Loudspeaker system to broadcast Starter's orders

Tape

Public not allowed around Starter's rostrum

The new start: Senior starter presses button hidden from jockeys' view

Release mechanism: Spring-loaded 'skate' lifts tape up and away at 45 degree angle to eliminate any possibility of horses or riders becoming entangled

Skate

Tape

Electric solenoid releases skate

SOURCES: The Jockey Club, Gill & Punter   © GRAPHIC NEWS

WINNERS ENCLOSURE

CHAPTER 9

Peace in our Time

Racing between the wars has often been described as 'The Golden Age of Racing'. In terms of talent, equine and human, it was. In terms of administration and villainy, less so, although much was done to improve the lot of the punter, with new grandstands, a clamp down on the extraordinary crime of welshing and the introduction of the Tote.

The origin of the word 'welsh' is unknown, but thankfully the activities of 'welshers' are also unknown, except by repute, to the modern generation of racegoers.

The modus operandi was easy. Prior to the introduction of betting tax in 1926, it was not required for bookmakers to be registered. Also, there were no pitch rules and it followed that any person could be an on-course bookmaker for a day, paying no more for admission than a punter and preferably operating on the free and unenclosed parts of the course. The Hill at Epsom or the Heath at Newmarket would be good examples. Once set up with a satchel slung in the manner of a schoolboy of the time containing say, five pounds, the welsher would commence to trade.

He would open a book, with a clerk noting the bets. If, for instance, a runner was being called at 6/4, he would offer 2/1, thus attracting custom. The punter investing, say, five shillings would be given a ticket with the 'name' – they were mostly 'noms-de-course' – of the bookmaker who would helpfully write the details of the transaction on the back of the ticket, including the name of the horse, the odds struck and the amount of the wager.

Well assured, the punter would go away to watch his selection win or lose. If the latter, the bookie happily kept the cash; if the former, and if the bookmakers liabilities exceeded the amount in the satchel, when the punter came to collect the winnings, he or she would find that either the bookmaker and clerk had vanished, or the ticket torn into small pieces by the bookie on presentation. Thus the bet could not be proven as the clerk was surprisingly unable to find an appropriate entry in his ledger.

Needless to say, punch-ups and even more vicious behaviour involving weapons became a frequent sight on the racecourse and the effect on innocent racegoers can only be imagined. Penalties for welshers, an offence officially described as 'stealing by means of a trick', were harsh enough, given the prison conditions of the time.

Three- or six-month sentences of hard labour with no remission and not even a meagre prisoner's wage were not uncommon, and worse for a persistent offender, but welshing became so chronic that the Jockey Club had to act in the absence of any effort by the racecourse executives, whose attitude can only be described as supine. Ring-keepers employed by the courses frequently ignored complaints and even allowed known welshers to return to the rings after they had been expelled.

What the sporting press of March 1925 described as a 'Flying Squad to aid the backer' was formed under the command of Major W P Wymer, formerly of Scotland Yard. This officer, operating from offices at 45 Wigmore Street, had under his command a team of ex-Scotland Yard men who knew 'the boys'. Two of them attended each meeting to assist the ring-keepers, who were still paid by the racecourses but drawn from a list of men licensed by the Jockey Club for the purpose.

Many convictions were secured, and by 1928 the *Sunday Chronicle* was reporting, 'We do not hear of many cases of welshing nowadays; certainly with his registration it is not necessary for a bookie to run away, but so long as there is a single case against him of non-payment he is stopped from standing up in the rings again.' The article went on to remind punters with a complaint to contact Major Wymer, adding, 'It is due to him and his staff that there had been such a big improvement in the rings.'

So, a victory for the Club, aided by the Exchequer. By 1928, the year of the *Sunday Chronicle* article, the betting tax introduced by Winston Churchill in 1926 was a dead duck, but the registration enforced by the Inland Revenue on bookmakers wishing to trade by way of a certificate issued by the Inspector of Taxes had the side effect of legalising the leggers.

The tax itself was a clumsy measure, ill-conceived and almost a design for evasion. Quite how such an experienced politician as Churchill thought that he as Chancellor could collect much revenue when all off-course cash betting was illegal, it is impossible to say. As a former Home Secretary, he must have known that evasion would be rife unless cash transactions away from the racecourse were as legitimate as credit betting. Not even the British Government could tax illegal gambling, any more than the American administration could charge duty on bootleg bathtub gin during the years of Prohibition.

As it was, the tax was levied on off-course credit bookmakers and on-course layers. Many of the former acted as 'launderers' for the illicit cash trade. The rates of tax were set at 2 per cent of turnover on racecourse bets with 3.5 per cent charged on the office transactions. The course bookie was sold tickets to be handed to the punter and recording the wagers in five colours: yellow for one shilling (five pence) bets, blue for 2 shillings, orange for

10 shillings, buff for £1 and for a hefty £5 stake buff with a green triangle superimposed. The bookmakers' registration cost £10 annually.

Naturally enough, the layers were incensed, many claiming that they would be driven out of business, a fear compounded by the pending introduction of the Totalisator, or 'Tote' referred to in some sections of the press as either the 'Mechanical bookie' or the 'Robot bookie'.

Both descriptions were misleading, as the Tote was a pool betting system and nothing to do with bookmaking and in any case the layers need not have feared. They staged the customary self-indulgence of a strike – at Windsor on Guy Fawkes Day – following the introduction of the tax on 1st November 1926. Their main beef was that although they had to pay the tax, they could not enforce their clients gambling debts at law. Furthermore, they were losing custom to the illegal street trade as the punters resented paying duty to the bookie, especially on losing bets.

THE BETTING SCENE

Long faces on Settling Day.

An Edwardian view of, amongst other things, a welshing bookmaker (bottom left) at Tarporley (Cheshire) races.

*Clockwise from top:
Jockeys were renowned
gamblers before the Jockey
Club put a stop to the
practice (officially).*

*The racegoer – a London
Transport poster of 1920
– a typical bookmaker of
the time.*

*Bookies in 1912 had a
rather more varied if not
flashy style of dress than
they do now.*

*Tic-tac men in full spate
passing information about
the latest odds around the
racecourse.*

*The first picture of the
Tote, Hamilton Park
September 30th 1929 –
although the very first Tote
was opened at Newmarket
on July 2nd of that year.*

*Posting the results borne by
carrier pidgoons outside
The Field's offices in
London.*

Apart from the illegal aspect, little has changed since. Gambling debts are still unenforceable and the bookmaker remains liable for the tax, simply passing it on to the punter as part of the transaction, usually a deduction from returns; so now that off-course betting is legal, the Treasury gets its revenue without fuss or bother.

Following the strike, which cost the Windsor executive £2,000 in lost gate money, the layers resumed at Newbury the next day, contenting themselves by forming a 'Betting Duty Reform Association' and lobbying Churchill for a repeal or at least an amendment to the tax.

The Chancellor was adamant that the tax must run for a full season to give it a decent trial, but in 1928 he brought the on-course duty down to 1 per cent and the off-course to 2 per cent. Although some turfites such as the Thoroughbred Breeders Association were optimistic enough to think that racing would benefit from the tax, both the Racecourse Association and the Jockey Club knew better. Racecourse attendances fell by 16 per cent between 1925 and 1927 and even allowing for such industrial catastrophes as the General Strike, the coincidence was too strong to ignore.

Churchill, who was a racing man through the influence of his father Lord Randolph, finally acknowledged that both the Club and the RCA were right. Not even a third of the anticipated revenue had been raised and he consigned his abortive tax to the mists of time, replacing it with a turnover levy on the new-fangled Tote and an utterly futile tax on bookmakers' telephones. Both measures were rightly repealed when Ramsey MacDonalds's second Labour Government was elected in June 1929.

The next thing to exercise bookmakers, ever anxious to protect their profits, was the introduction of the Totalisator in 1929. This was essentially the brainchild of Lord Hamilton of Dalzell and his close friend and associate Brigadier-General Sir Loftus Bates, an experienced and skilful racecourse administrator.

The idea sprang from the report of a Jockey Club committee chaired by Lord Hamilton in 1919. The main consideration was new facilities for the future administration of the Turf. Conditions on racecourses were highlighted and it was thought desirable that some tracks should amalgamate, the overall cost of going to the races lowered and better accommodation provided, in particular for female racegoers.

The report, like so many others commissioned by the Jockey Club, was imaginative and innovative, but the Club, as so often has been the case in the past, failed to act on the most important issues, leaving the racecourses to play their maverick role in the structure of racing. Amalgamation was watered down by the considerations of 'local opinion' while the charges for admission and the standards of comfort remained disproportionate.

Like the bookies, the racecourse executives pleaded poverty and the Tote, conceived as a non-profit-making organisation with a substantial proportion of its income returned to racing, seemed the answer. Churchill's tax had failed to wring much out of the layers, who still made no contribution to the sport off which they leeched their profits.

The Tote was not a new idea; indeed it had been mooted by the industry as early as 1916, but at that time Britain was at war and the Jockey Club rightly concluded that there were more important matters for the Government to consider than the financing of the 'great triviality'.

Lord Hamilton, as Senior Steward, raised the issue again in a speech to the Gimcrack Club in 1927. It was clear that betting should contribute to the upkeep of racing and a meeting between the Jockey Club, the National Hunt Committee and the National Coursing Club resulted in an approach to Churchill, who was not surprisingly in a receptive mood. He could not allocate any time for a Government sponsored Bill to set up the Tote, but agreed to give time and support to a Private Members Bill, if fortunate in the usual draw.

Accordingly, the Jockey Club instructed their lawyers to draft a Bill. As luck would have it, one of the Bill's sponsors, Major (later Sir) Ralph Glyn, who represented Abingdon as a Tory MP, drew a place in the ballot.

So far, so good; but it was far from the end of the story. The moralists whom Churchill had rightly feared while introducing his doomed tax legislation formed an unholy alliance with Labour members to fight the Bill. It is one of the paradoxes and hypocrisies of socialist philosophy that although left-wing dogma demands equality and negates private enterprise, throughout Parliamentary history Labour have consistently sided with bookmakers who some might consider to be the very epitome of the self-interested entrepreneurs.

The Bill just scrambled to a second reading and at the Committee stage the minutiae obviously necessary to draft such detailed legislation gave ample opportunity to those opponents of the Bill skilled in tactical obstruction and plain old-fashioned filibustering; the legislation scraped through just before the House rose for the summer recess. The Lords found no difficulties and the Racecourse Betting Bill was entered on the Statute Book.

As originally conceived by Lord Hamilton and Sir Loftus, the administration of the Tote would have been in the hands of the Jockey Club and the National Hunt Committee, thus ensuring control of both operation and cash flow for the immediate benefit of racing. However, one of the concessions Major Glyn and his supporters had to make to ensure the passage of the Bill was the creation of a statutory body to run the Tote, to be known as the Racecourse Betting Control Board and responsible to Parliament.

The Government was heavily represented on the Board with five of the twelve members, including the Chairman and one other appointed by the Home Secretary and representatives of the Exchequer, the Scottish Office and the Ministry of Agriculture. The Jockey Club had three seats, the National Hunt Committee two, while the Racecourse Association and Tattersalls Committee occupied one each.

The terms of the Board's duties were clearly stated: after taxation and running costs had been covered, plus donations to charities, all profits remaining were to be devoted to 'improvement of the breeds of horses the sport of horseracing and veterinary science and education'.

On the bookmakers' side of the Betting Bill, the admission charge for racecourse layers was to be limited to five times the public's payment for use of the same enclosure and the Board had the responsibility of seeing that the bookies and the Tote enjoyed equal facilities.

An overdraft of two million pounds was obtained from a leading bank. Given the economic situation prevailing at the time, the chairman of the bank (or perhaps it was the manager of the Tooting Branch, SW) was either the biggest racing fan since Edward VII or the greatest optimist since Icarus. Either way, the money was there and the Tote was launched simultaneously at Sir Loftus Bates's course, Carlisle and Newmarket on 2nd July 1929. Newmarket's first race was fifteen minutes earlier than the Northumberland course and so had the honour of declaring the first dividend: 80s. 6d to a 2 shilling stake on Humcoat ridden by Harry Wragg.

In his speech to the Gimcrack Club at a dinner presided over by the centenarian James Melrose in November 1928, Lord Dewar welcomed the Bill, remarking, 'The Totalisator is not a matter of speculative hypothesis – it combines the principles, recourses and potentialities which have proved vital to the progressive prosperity of horseracing and breeding in other countries where it is in operation and it has proved successful.' Acknowledging that the machine would not be perfect, Lord Dewar advocated patience, observing, 'The Tote will bring things home to you that you have never seen before, as your laundry man sometimes does, and if you want credit from the Tote, you will find it colder than a banker's heart.'

In fact, a certain amount of pessimism was justified. Although the Tote could not welsh and with 2 shilling units and place only betting appealed to the small punter, especially women who did not wish to mix in the raucous hurly-burly of the ring, it had little interest for professionals or heavy backers who simply 'did' their own money by depressing the dividend by the sheer weight of their stakes. Most punters preferred the bookie, who settled at known odds taken, as opposed to the indeterminate dividend based on the number of successful tickets in the pool. The Tote was never to gain more than 3-6 per cent share of the betting market.

Matters have slightly improved under the inspired chairmanship of Lord Wyatt and of course the 'Nanny Goat' has had a credit business since 1931. It was not until 1933 that the Tote found itself in surplus and this was only £9,841 on a turnover of nearly £4.5 million. However, by the outbreak of war in 1939, the surplus was running at over eighteen times as much. As the economy recovered, so did the 'Nanny'. Never intended as a monopoly, it nonetheless provided funds for improved prize money, amenities, technical innovations such as the photo-finish and enhanced conditions for stable staff, stabling, dope-testing, veterinary services and local stewarding. In 1938, off-course betting with the Tote amounted to £2.5 million. The legal betting alone with off-track bookmaking firms came to approximately £85 million, but not one penny piece of the layers' profits found its way towards the improvement or preservation of the sport on which they were dependent.

Lord Hamilton of Dalzell's dream had come true, at least in part. A member of the Jockey Club for fifty-four years, he was one of the finest racing administrators of the inter-war period, a Steward for seven years and Senior Steward for three. Possessed of a progressive mind coupled with the rare ability to think ahead, his far-sightedness served the Club and racing well.

Formerly a major in the Scots Guards, Lord Hamilton was a close friend of King George V and served as His Majesty's Representative at Royal Ascot between 1934 and 1945, but he will be best remembered as a reformer of the Turf.

Although succeeding in the virtual elimination of welshers, the Jockey Club could do little to prevent the menace of pick-pockets on racecourses which continues to this day. Indeed, one of the early objections to the Tote was that as it was cash only on-course, people seen to be drawing winnings would be especially vulnerable to 'the dips'.

Within the confines of the course, the Club did its best to deal with race gangs, who were really nothing to do with racing at all, but bands of criminals operating protection rackets against bookmakers in addition to the usual terrorising of pubs, shops, off-licences and restaurants. Unfortunately, the Jockey Club had no legal powers to exclude wrongdoers from the courses. The major problem was not so much the activities of the gangs on the tracks, hideous as they were to the ordinary racegoers, witnessing fights in which the combatants used weaponry including hammers, knives and 'cut-throat' razors, but the continuation of the internecine warfare outside or in the proximity of the tracks, areas over which neither the Club nor the racecourse executives had any control.

The protection system operated by the gangs, who principally emanated from London, Birmingham and Sheffield, a convenient and not entirely coincidental regional division, was simple enough. The chief threat to bookmakers was razor-slashing, a technique perfected by various Italian gangsters based in London and dedicated to improving the skills taught to them as apprentices in East End barbers' shops. Thus armed, the gang's front men told the bookmaker that the list of runners, normally priced at one shilling, would be sold to them at five shillings. 'Ground money' was also demanded, ranging from £2 to £20 for the privilege of standing unmolested on a particular spot.

Non-compliance would result in the bookie's stool and joint being knocked over, his satchel and money stolen, or ultimately a vicious attack as he left the end of the meeting; few witnesses could be found who were willing to give evidence.

Following an affray outside the Embassy Club in Brighton in August 1925, an unhappy gentleman called Isiah Elboz whose face was bandaged and carried his left arm in a sling, could not stand in court two days later and had to be seated in the witness box. Despite losing a great deal of blood, Elboz could not remember how he acquired a wound on his face, or the wound on his arm, or indeed anything to do with the assault, although his alleged assailant, Sidney Payne, was well known to him. As the clearly intimidated Elboz refused to speak the court had no option but to release Payne.

The police were far from happy, as they were frequently attacked when they attempted to break up the warring factions. In May 1925, two brothers, Wilfred and Lawrence Fowler, members of the 'Park' mob of Sheffield, used a poker and a razor to murder William Plummer, a rival race-gangster. The Fowlers' violent progress was duly halted by entanglement with a loop of hempen rope suspended over a well-oiled trap door. Consequently, the Home Secretary who authorised the death warrant, Sir William Joynson-Hicks, took action by rapidly increasing the strength of policing on the race gangs' home 'patches' and on the racecourses.

Police strength and presence is usually an effective deterrent and prevention is better than cure, a philosophy to which our hard-pressed constabulary would doubtless subscribe today, assuming that their slender resources and a weak Criminal Justice Act allow.

So effective was the clamp-down that at the 1925 Annual Dinner of the Bookmakers Protection Association, which had been formed in 1921, the speakers were able to relax and rejoice in the knowledge that the foul tide of criminal flotsam was finally ebbing. The Jockey Club were congratulated for their work and especially Major Wymer and his racecourse redcaps. Suitably soothed, the layers and their ladies danced the night away at the Holborn Restaurant to the music of Jessie Widon and her orchestra.

However, the gangs were not defeated yet. At a hoods' convention held at an East End night club in March 1926 the three most powerful mobs, London, Sheffield and Birmingham, with four delegates from each, met with the Cheshire gang. The London element were representing the 'Sabini', the 'Aldgate', the 'Hoxton' and the 'Nile'.

It sounds like a scene from a Chevey novel or a Warner Brothers crime movie, but this was real life. The gangs agreed to end their own feuds in order to wage a more effective war on the racegoing public. Under the chairmanship of the usual 'Mr Big' whose anonymity also cloaked a front of healthy respectability, demarcation lines were drawn with each gang given the exclusive right to extort 'tributes' from the bookmakers operating in their respective territories. Interestingly, Ascot was excluded from the list of course to be 'worked' on the grounds that it would be to difficult to get in to the various enclosures. Plus ça change… it's hard to beat an Ascot gateman today, and long may that be so.

But by now the gangs' stars were truly on the wane and, apart from the occasional bloody brawl, peace returned to the racecourse during the 'thirties.

Meanwhile, on the racing front, Lord Durham placed a notice in the *Calendar* of 9th April 1925 prior to the meeting of the Jockey Club due to take place the first Spring Week. His object was to ask the Club to abolish the existing system under which sentences passed on offenders by the Turf authorities of other countries became automatically operative in England under the reciprocal agreements which the Club had with racing bodies elsewhere.

This was, and fortunately remains, a system which is very important to the sport worldwide. Lord Durham's motion was motivated by the case of one C Rhodes, apprenticed to R G Pickering at Newmarket, who made an absolute nonsense of a ride at the Curragh on an eight-year-old mare, Grove Fairy, trained by Harvey Leader. The Stewards of the Irish Turf Club, suspecting chicanery, withdrew Rhodes's licence and automatically Rhodes was warned off in Britain.

George Lambton and Lord Durham thought that a considerable injustice had been done to Rhodes, as it was possible that his conduct was incompetent rather than criminal, but that was no reason to tamper with the greater issue and revoke a reasonable, practical and workable reciprocal agreement. The whole thing smacked a little of the Newmarket mafia and the Club voted down Durham's motion.

The Jockey Club members caricatured.

Another factor which is relevant today was raised by Lord Ronaldshay, later second Marquis of Zetland, at the Gimcrack Dinner in 1928. One of Stanley Wooton's apprentices, N Carroll, had been warned off after Wooton had reported him for selling stable information to bookmakers. As with disciplinary hearings today, the matter was dealt with by the Stewards in camera, with the usual bald statement of the outcome in the *Calendar*.

Carroll's version was that he had been disqualified from riding after talking 'indiscreetly' to a friend about the outcome of a trial, although the bookmaker concerned had also been warned off.

The press latched on to the old 'Star Chamber' theme demanding the evidence and even access to disciplinary hearings. Nowadays, with legal representation on both sides, matters are more open and probably better justice is dispensed, but there can be no doubt that public tribunals would protract the length of the enquiry

and certainly inhibit witnesses who could well be prosecuted in the courts if committing, for instance, perjury. The Jockey Club are merely the regulatory body of a sport and a better one than many – the ruling bodies of football, cricket and tennis spring to mind – and there is an appeal system. If still unhappy, the aggrieved always have recourse to the Courts of Britain.

Nonetheless, the blunt instrument of warning-off with no redress was extremely harsh and a system of suspensions, even for major offences such as apply today, would have been better in the interest of justice – to say nothing of the livelihood of the offender.

It was, of course, a matter of judgement. The Stewards had the power to suspend if they wished to exercise their discretion, but one area in which they had little option was doping, although the original rule quoted in Chapter 7 had by now been amended to read:

> If in any case it shall be found that any drug or stimulant has been administered to a horse for the purpose of affecting its speed in a race, the licence of the trainer of the horse shall be withdrawn and he shall be declared a disqualified person.

In 1930, Charles Chapman trained a horse called Don Pat at his yard in Sussex. After the six-year-old had won the Bedfont Plate High Weight Handicap at Kempton, he tested positive for a fairly hefty quantity of caffeine.

Inevitably, Chapman was warned-off under the blanket or 'catch-all' rule that the trainer was responsible, although it was obviously possible that the doping had been done by a third party. Unfortunately, the published decision of the Stewards in the *Calendar* implied that Chapman might have administered the caffeine himself.

Lead by *The Times*, which then claimed to be 'The Organ of the Nation', a slogan which always sounded slightly pornographic, the press had a field day and before long it was clear that the public had the impression that Chapman was guilty of fraud. Not only had he lost his stable and his living, but he was regarded as a criminal.

No appeal to the Club members in respect of the decision was possible, and so Charles Chapman sued for libel against the Stewards and *The Times*, the first paper to repeat the statement in the *Calendar*.

It was a brave act. On the face of it the Stewards, the Lords Rosebery, Ellesmere and Harewood had acted correctly under the Rules and Chapman pinned his hopes on convincing the jury that the wording of the decision as published was capable of meaning that he personally doped the horse.

His legal team were led by Sir Patrick Hastings, QC and Hastings decided that the best ploy was to ask for substantial damages as the Jockey Club must have realised the false impression fermented by the press for the benefit of a gullible public, but had done nothing to erase or correct that impression. In the witness box, Chapman pursued this line, accepting the outcome of the

Stewards' Inquiry where he said he had been treated with complete fairness, complaining only of the implications against his integrity, a slur on his character which the Club had not troubled to remove.

When Hastings came to cross-examine the Stewards he stressed the hardship done to Chapman and asked why such hardship had not been relieved when it was clearly within their powers to do so, and they must have known the harm done to his client by the various newspaper articles.

Almost laughably, all three Stewards claimed not to have read them. Now, it is indeed hard to imagine the 6th Earl of Rosebery curled up at the Turf Club with a copy of the *Daily Mirror*, or the *News of the World*, but it is impossible to believe that neither he, nor Lord Ellesmere, nor Lord Harewood did not read *The Times*.

The defence, namely that the decision was valid and true, that under the Rules Chapman automatically agreed to the publication of the decision in the *Calendar* and so the Stewards were therefore privileged, did not wash with the judge, Mr Justice Horridge, who apparently indulged in the odd foray to Hurst Park, Kempton and Sandown and asked the jury to decide on the basis that the wording of the decision meant that Chapman was party to the doping of Don Pat. The twelve men and true decided that this was so and awarded the plaintiff £13,000 damages against the Stewards and Weatherby's in respect of the publication in the *Calendar* and £3,000 against *The Times*.

This was a dangerous precedent for the Jockey Club and, at the subsequent appeal, the court decided that the Club was privileged as were Weatherby's and the verdict against them quashed, but no such privilege existed for *The Times*. A retrial of the case against the newspaper was ordered but the matter settled out of court.

Charles Chapman's honour was vindicated and it was a close call for the Club. Doubtless the lesson was well learned and would certainly not have

In 1935, after the Jockey Club headquarters at Newmarket had been largely rebuilt, a building at the back – luckily part of the old section – caught fire.

been lost on Lord Rosebery, who was not only to prove to be a fine administrator in the best Bentinck/Bunbury/ Rous tradition but was just coming into his own as an owner-breeder having inherited the Mentmore Stud from his father in 1929. He was a Steward from 1929 to 1932 and again from 1945 to 1948, being Senior Steward in both ultimate years.

An all-round sportsman – as Lord Dalmeny he captained Surrey from 1905 to 1907 while he was also Liberal MP for the county of Edinburgh, a combination of talents unthinkable nowadays – his political experience stood him in good stead during the war when he was Regional Commissioner for Civil Defence in Scotland from 1941, later serving as Secretary of State for Scotland in 1945. His affection for Edinburgh never diminished and despite a career as an owner which yielded hundreds of winners mostly trained by Sir Jack Jarvis and later by Doug Smith and Bruce Hobbs, including five classic successes, the little gaff track at Musselborough remained close to Rosebery's heart.

Father and son: the Lords Rosebery and Dalmeny at Edinburgh – names synonymous with the Turf. The sixth Earl was a brilliant cricketer, polo player and rider to hounds in his youth and was for over forty years one of the most active members of the Jockey Club made notable by shrewdness and formidable power of repartee.

When it was threatened with closure following the withdrawal of financial support by the Levy Board in 1963, he was having none of it. With all the vigour of a former forcing bat, first class rider to hounds and polo player of international standard, together with his experience of dealing with irascible Field Marshals gained during his service on the staff or Lord Allenby between 1914–18, he told the Chairman of the Levy Board, Field Marshal Lord Harding, his precise views. The Board duly relented and awarded £700 per day prize money and £2,000 towards course improvements.

Rosebery was brought up in the tradition of public service; his father was a Prime Minister. Racing owes much to such patricians with real as opposed to synthetic social conscience. When Rosebery died in 1974, he carried with him the admiration and affection of the racing world; but this was thankfully a long way off when Jack Jarvis prepared Rosebery's Two Thousand Guineas and Derby winner Blue Peter to win the Triple Crown with the 1939 St Leger. The race was never to be run.

A former house-painter, designer of greetings cards and some time corporal in the Austrian army suffering from extreme body odour decided to intervene. Yet again, there was 'a Treaty too far', this time signed at Munich in 1938. In 1919 the French war commander Marshal Foch had described the Treaty of Versailles as 'a twenty years truce'; how right he was.

Lord Lonsdale as Senior Steward of the Jockey Club drives down to Epsom in the year of his election 1926, with cases of Moet & Chandon and others including the Earl of Derby, George Lambton his trainer (inside) and Jimmy de Rothschild (clinging to the back).

CHAPTER 10

War and Peace

The truce ended on 3rd September, 1939. As in 1914, a 'phoney war' period ensued, presumably while the politicians slowly realised the horror of their commitment and the military gazed with equal dismay on their armoury of ageing tanks, stringbag aircraft and antique battleships, betrayed as ever by the politico's peacetime economic policy of 'butter, not guns'.

Racing was severely restricted as it had been during the First World War. The usual objections ranging from unpatriotic conduct to the shortage of petrol, and a break in racing between June and September 1940 enabled opponents of wartime racing to indulge in a stream of protests, headed by a leading article in *The Times* which asserted that there would be 'widespread resentment' if racing were resumed.

It was admittedly a period which encompassed the fall of France, the defeat of the British Expeditionary Force and the subsequent debacle of Dunkirk, the Blitz and the Battle of Britain, but nonetheless Lord Ilchester, who had recently retired as Senior Steward and was ably supported by George Lambton, successfully silenced most of the outcry in letters to 'The Organ of the Nation'. However, the organ was evidently in a virile mood and the following year published a collection of correspondence under the heading 'Why Racing?'

It has been said that patriotism is the last refuge of a scoundrel; one might add that 'public opinion' is the last excuse of the incompetent politician. Mr Emmanuel Shinwell (later Lord Shinwell) fell back on the cliché yet again when he spoke in the Commons on behalf of Labour Party colleagues hostile to the sport which they regarded, according to *Hansard*, as 'an insane and unseemly spectacle'.

This description presumably did not cover such proletarian pastimes as Association football matches and greyhound racing, which were allowed to continue unabated. In any case 'Manny' and his parliamentary chums were informed at Question Time that their claim for oats fed to racehorses be given instead to poultry, to increase the egg supply for hungry workers, would result in an additional output of one egg per head of the population in four years.

A brilliant piece of research by the Ministry of Food; and while Mr Shinwell and his colleagues pondered the ideological implications for the masses, the punters were already voting with their feet. Doubtless happy enough with powdered egg, the nation flocked in droves to witness substitute Derbies at Newmarket and other events within the restricted Calendar. Racing provided rest, recuperation and a day in the fresh air away from the stink of fire bombs, dirt, dust, death and the wail of the sirens. They did not find the spectacle of racing either insane or unseemly.

Lord Shinwell, scourge of wartime racing, on the occasion of the launching of his memoirs. Lord Home made the speech.

As always, there was a quid pro quo. The Jockey Club, with Lord Sefton as Senior Steward, agreed to encourage owners to dispose of moderate stock, especially geldings, and it was decided after talks with the Ministry of Agriculture that the broodmare population should be reduced by 25 per cent.

Racing went ahead at several courses: Windsor, Newmarket, Salisbury, Pontefract, Thirsk, Manchester, Stockton, Ascot and Catterick were all allocated fixtures at various times, subject to the menacing rider in *Horses in Training* which read, 'It must be realised that altered circumstances may necessitate the abandonment of fixtures even at the shortest notice.' And they were.

Cheltenham and one or two other tracks such as Wetherby and Worcester struggled on with National Hunt racing for a year or so, but finally capitulated and winter racing did not resume properly until 1946. However, the important issue was to maintain what we would now call 'pattern' racing with a few handicaps thrown in to keep the punters' interest alive.

Accordingly, the Queen Mary Stakes was run throughout the war – at

Newmarket after 1940. The Molecomb Stakes and the Sussex Stakes were run at the July Course in 1941 and following the closure of York the Nunthorpe Stakes also took place at HQ in 1942, 1943 and 1944.

Windsor featured strongly. Not only did this course stage the substitute Stewards' Cup from 1942 to 1945, but also the July Stakes in 1943 and 1944. The quality of the race was not diluted even if the 1943 event had to be run in two divisions for the sake of safety on Windsor's tricky figure-of-eight course. Nineteen horses contested Division One, and nine took part in Division Two.

The 'Newmarket Cesarewitch' was run over two miles and 24 yards of the summer course, which was truncated by military use. The classics were staged on the July Course, with the usual exception of the St Leger. Three runnings, 1942, '43 and '44, all took place at HQ but the 1940 version was run at Thirsk on 23rd November (the last day of the season), the 1941 event was at Manchester and York placed host in 1945.

It was a sad blow to the racing world in 1942 when Lord Glanely was killed in an air raid on Weston-super-Mare of all places. Probably the wretched German was discharging the remainder of his bomb load following an attack on the Bristol docks. Glanely, a former shipping clerk, self-made millionaire and member of the Jockey Club, was loved by all classes of racegoer, who affectionately dubbed him 'Old Guts and Gaiters'.

One of the founders of Chepstow racecourse, where he was not ashamed to direct the traffic leaving the course, Lord Glanely recorded his first winner in 1909, won six classic races including Grand Parade's Derby in 1919, and his election to the Club in 1929 was valued by him almost as much as his peerage, coming as he did from a much humbler walk of life than most of his fellow members. He was not only a breeder on a massive scale, but also spent freely at the yearling sales. Politically astute, he successfully appealed to the House of Lords in 1933 to abolish the taxation on stallion fees. His last classic winner was Dancing Time in the 1941 Thousand Guineas, home-bred and ridden by Dick Perryman.

The administration of racing was naturally tempered by the demands of the war. The Senior Steward, Lord Sefton, had to combine his duties as an officer in the Royal Horse Guards with making decisions such as those involving a drastic reduction in the number of horses in training. In 1942, the Club announced that horses of five years old and upwards would not be eligible to run in handicaps after 1st June. It was a harsh decision, as it meant that some animals had been omitted from the list of horses for which applications for rations had been made to the Ministry of Agriculture.

This severe measure amounted to a death sentence for many horses, but it was justified by circumstances unthinkable in the soft, cushioned society of today. It also impressed the Government as to the Jockey Club's determination to keep the promise that the racehorse population would be culled.

In 1943, racing was down to the bare bones. Many blamed Sefton, an

The young 6th Duke of Portland as Master of the Horse – a popular owner who became one of the Club's oldest members.

aloof aristo of the old school, but his fellow Stewards, led by Lord Rosebery, pointed out that there was little more that Sefton could do, given the civil servants and socialist MP's breathing down his neck.

In the same year, another distinguished member kept his date with St Peter: the Duke of Portland, a throwback to the last century and the man who bought St Simon. Portland was one of the Club's oldest members; he owned and bred eleven classic winners and was the author of two books, *Memoirs of Racing and Hunting* (1935) and the somewhat surprisingly if charmingly entitled, *Men, Women and Things* (1937). The Duke was 86, and for many years had distanced himself from Turf affairs.

The image of wartime racing was given a tremendous boost by the success of King George VI during the 1942 season. The King, although he had been elected to the Jockey Club when Duke of York in 1921, could hardly be described as a racing man but he sustained the regal interest in the Turf fostered by his grandfather and father. In 1942 the King won the Two Thousand Guineas with Big Game and Sun Chariot, after a little coaxing, took the Thousand Guineas, the Oaks and the St Leger.

The young 6th Duke of Portland as Master of the Horse – a popular owner who became one of the Club's oldest members.

His Majesty was naturally disappointed when denied a nap hand after Big Game had failed in the Derby behind Watling Street, but four out of five wasn't bad and the premiere classic has always proved elusive to reigning monarchs – with the exception of Edward VII.

It was evident to many members of the Club that peace would bring a social change comparable to that following the 1914–18 conflict. Such is the way of war and the future, assuming victory, always uncertain. Racing had to know what it was doing and formulate a policy to see it through the immediate post-war years.

A committee was formed in 1941, 'To consider the whole future of racing in general, and in particular with reference to the encouragement of owners and greater comfort and convenience of the public.' Lord Ilchester, a former Senior Steward, took the chair and the other members were the Duke of Norfolk and the Lords Harewood, Zetland, Portal and Sir Humphrey de Trafford.

Lord Glanely owner and breeder on a lavish scale between the wars. Known as 'Guts and Gaiters' he was killed in a 1942 air raid. Here he's with a youthful Gordon Richards

All were experienced Turf administrators, with the young Turk being Bernard Norfolk, a man of ideas on the future of racing; since he had masterminded the Coronation of King George VI in the extraordinary circumstances following the Abdication crisis, he was well able to look at the long term on a 'nuts and bolts' basis.

The demands of wartime life prevented the committee from delivering their report until 1943. In the light of subsequent events, it is clear that the recommendations should have been implemented, not only to illustrate that the Club desired a clean break with the past, but to guide the sport into modern times. As has been noted before, the Jockey Club were good at commissioning committees to report on the state of racing, but then largely ignored the findings and advice; this philosophy set back progress by more than four decades.

The committee concluded that racing in Britain was in decline, and analysed in some depth the respective situations of the owner, the horse and the racegoing public along with the racecourse executives.

The latter emerged badly. The report stated: 'Racecourse Executives, with a few exceptions, have shown little disposition to cater for the individual – man or woman – outside of the fringe of those directly concerned with the business of racing. Yet from this reservoir must be drawn the increased attendances which we seek, for from it must come a large part of the new money required to bring about the improvements which are called for, particularly during the early years of reorganisation.'

Going on to plea for the modernisation of facilities, the report added: 'We would urge that now is the time when changes will be most easily effected.'

History has shown that far from the 'new money' being attracted from and being used on behalf of the racegoer, it was gleaned from corporate hospitality and lavished on fair weather punters. The report went on to complete its message by indicating that some tracks were redundant and should be abolished while pointing out that only Stockton, York, Salisbury, Newmarket and Ascot were run as non-profit-making ventures.

The idea behind this thinking was that the Jockey Club should form a trust 'to obtain the ownership of a number of racecourses which would be run by the Club, not for the benefit of directors and shareholders, but for the benefit of racing and the racing public as a whole.'

This eminently sensible suggestion was supported by the Jockey Club but fell foul of Treasury regulations in respect of capital issues. Thus, a reform which could and should have been implemented in 1944 did not in fact come into being until 1964, when the Racecourse Holdings Trust was established to ensure the future of Cheltenham. The Trust now controls twelve racecourses including such important venues as Aintree, Epsom, Sandown, Haydock and Kempton in addition to the home of steeplechasing.

In the intervening twenty-odd years, racecourses were culled by commercial pressures, principally land speculation involving inner-city tracks such as Birmingham and Manchester. These were followed by Newport, Hurst Park,

Lewes, Lincoln and Woore. Wye, Lanark and Alexandra Park (the latter unlamented) followed in the 1970s while the last course to close was Stockton *alias* Tees-side Park in 1981.

This could perhaps be regarded as 'natural wastage' in the modern jargon, but there can be little doubt that a major chance for change fell by the wayside, and the truth became apparent yet again nearly three decades later in June 1969 as expressed in a report by a working party chaired by Sir Rex (later Lord) Cohen. The subject was racecourse management.

If one looks at racing in theatrical terms, the racecourse is the stage on which the performers, human and equine, hopefully hold the audience in thrall. As in the theatre, the public will be largely ignorant of the trials and tribulations of rehearsals, in our analogy equated to the training grounds, or the personal lives of the riders entrusted with the punters' cash. Jockeys, like actors, can have headaches, hangovers and tax demands as well as a triumphant performance and leavened by the bitterness of failure and injury. The track is the 10 per cent tip of the racing iceberg, where reputations are made and lost and the Rules applied to govern the biggest 'money sport' in the world. It follows that the administrative responsibility of the racecourses is very considerable.

The Cohen report makes it clear that the running of courses could not be regarded in any light other than 'the management of a commercial enterprise in the entertainment industry'. The report concluded that this aspect should be the province of a properly trained racecourse manager, leaving the Clerk of the Course, re-titled 'Clerk to the Races' to concentrate on running the racing element. This was a reasonable conclusion bearing in mind that the Clerk is the only person employed by the course who is licensed by the Jockey Club. His contribution to the show-biz side would be the framing of entertaining and attractive races.

To return to the theatrical comparison, the manager would look after the 'bricks and mortar' of the playhouse including bars, lavatories, restaurants and other essential facilities, while the Clerk of the Course attended to the plays and players in the drama/comedy/farce; a race may be any of those things remembering that there is no script (or there should not be).

Generally speaking, this has not happened. Since the Cohen report, the commercial pressures on racecourses and therefore Clerks have increased many fold, notably in the field of finding sponsorship. Although racecourses now enjoy a considerable income from non-racing activities as advocated by Cohen – several utilising grandstands built by way of Levy Board interest-free loans the average racegoer paying his or her money at the gate finds inadequate facilities, especially for viewing; the corporate entertainment boxes take up the best vantage points. Racing is not the only sport to suffer from the corporate tail wagging the genuine and knowledgeable supporting 'dog' to the latter's disadvantage.

Cohen defined the general public 'to whom the racecourses were selling' in three categories: the habitual racegoer, the occasional racegoer and the non-racegoer, going on to state that, 'Whilst the habitual racegoer clearly wants reasonable facilities, there is no need to sell racing to him. We must therefore concentrate on the occasional racegoer to make him come more often and the non-racegoer to interest him in the sport.'

Inevitably, it is the habitual racegoer who has lost out; he or she were taken for granted and for the non-racegoer read 'corporate hospitality recipient'. Habitual, including professional racegoing, is largely confined to weekdays, and such people rarely venture forth on Saturdays and Bank Holidays. It remains to be seen if they are attracted by Sunday racing, but on past experience this is unlikely.

Indeed, it may well be that in the not too distant future, the habitual racegoer may become a protected species, as the numbers of those who go racing to see and bet on races slowly vanish under the tidal wave of Bouncy Castles and other unrelated distractions.

Twenty-five years on from the Cohen report more serious problems had manifested themselves. In 1985 the Racecourse Association commissioned a working party to report on declining standards of crowd behaviour. It was a classic case of bolting the door after the horse had fled, and in 1988 a man was killed during a brawl on the July course at Newmarket; this followed disgraceful scenes on the Rowley on 2,000 Guineas day, and a new working party was convened by the RCA. However, the recommendations did little more than reinforce most of the guidelines already in place.

The report of the original working party recommended restrictions on drinking but apart from such minor rules as prohibiting the taking of glasses of alcoholic beverages from bars, the importation of drinks and the early closing of bars on 'busy days', things are not very different today than in 1985.

The courses appeared to accept little blame and the approach was almost flippant, with dismissive references to outbursts of temper at vicarage choir practice and mythical colonels suffering apoplexy at the sight of improperly dressed racegoers, the degree of choleric reaction apparently depending on which war the officer fought in.

The caterers came in for some stick, as the report implies that tables not cleared of bottles, glasses and other debris, constitute some incitement to riot. The report also stated the obvious when observing that group bookings arriving by coach were already 'well primed' in the alcoholic sense. The fact remains that, given the general decline in behavioural standards of all classes of society since the early sixties which the report admits, there can be no final solution except a prohibition on drinking at racecourses, as applies to football grounds.

The report emphasises that, at the time, there was little danger to horse or rider from intoxicated punters, but also admitted that such an eventuality would be impossible to prevent. The truth of this was well proven when a drunken lout ran out in front of Papago, a tail ender in the Ribblesdale Stakes

German POWs rather than the runners being paraded at Kempton.

at Royal Ascot in 1994, an incident which could easily have cost the life of her jockey, Michael Kinane, and the filly as well.

In this context, the author is reminded of a 'busy' day at a major north-western racecourse. Many homeward bound racegoers were giving a good impression of the late comedian Freddie Frinton in his 'drunk hanging onto a lamp-post' sketch. The next day the racecourse executive proudly announced that only one punter had been apprehended for drunkenness on the course. The police confirmed that forty-three racegoers had been taken into custody just outside the gates following the last race and subsequently convicted of being drunk and disorderly.

It will always be difficult to balance the prosperity of the courses against the essential continuance of the sport, regardless of gimmicks or commercial pressures. 'The play's the thing', and the 'conscience of the King' must rule over such important matters as husbandry of the Turf, the proper maintenance of running rails, starting equipment, stable blocks, facilities for stable staff and their horses, weighing rooms, ambulances, judge's boxes and the integrity services, ie photo-finish cameras, camera patrol etc. which should take precedence over hospitality tents, crêches and children's play areas, desirable though they may be; and an overriding consideration must be for crowd safety measures.

The Cohen report was far reaching and far sighted. It is to be regretted that its recommendations were not universally adopted and even today the Jockey Club still regards crowd control as the responsibility of the racecourse, although help and advice is given on such matters as policing.

The Club's view in the late nineties is that ideally the Clerk of the Course should, whenever possible, be relieved of the burden of managing the track and that the racecourse manager should not impinge on the duties of the Clerk and vice-versa, while more assistant Clerks should be appointed to this end.

The wartime Derby run at Newmarket was an informal affair.

Although the Racecourse Committee is not a Standing Committee of the Jockey Club, it licences racecourses and vets the financial standing of racecourse owners. However, insofar as any licence to operate can be withdrawn if specified standards are not met, the Club appears to have surprisingly little clout in such an important area, save for the tracks controlled by Racecourse Holdings Trust, which is a Jockey Club subsidiary.

To return briefly to the years of conflict, it must be remembered that racing itself was not the only element of the sport to face the realities of total war. It was no joke to live and work in the inner cities of Britain during the height of the Blitz, as the author can testify. In April 1941, Weatherby's office in Cavendish Square suffered bomb damage, mostly broken glass, which was normal and in this case included the typing pool, a lavatory window and 'the roof over Lavel's desk' which was 'slightly misplaced'.

The whole damage cost £14.19s.0d which was added to a previous claim, amount unknown. Two years later, in April 1943, a note from Weatherby's to the estate agent said with masterly understatement, 'Some time has elapsed since your call regarding the work we asked you to put in hand and we should be glad to know, as time is getting on, if you can report progress.' The writer added, somewhat wistfully, 'No builder has yet called.'

However, by October 1943, all was well and a triumphant receipt was issued acknowledging a cheque from the War Damage Commission for £87.16s.2d. Presumably Lavel was able to return to his desk, God was in His Heaven and all was right with the world. Hitler simply did not know who he was taking on in 1939.

CHAPTER 11

The Watershed Years

When Roger Mortimer completed his history of the Club in 1957, the world was a very different place. It was the winding down of an era when the fictional James Bond and the real life John Tyrrel could park their Le Mans Bentley (Bond) and Austin A35 (Tyrrel) outside their flats in Chelsea (Royal Avenue for Bond, Hospital Road for Tyrrel) with the reasonable certainty that the vehicles would not only be in place in the morning, but also free from vandalism.

The nineteen-sixties spawned a social revolution unequalled since the industrial upheavals of the mid-nineteenth century. It is interesting to reflect on how all periods of repression are followed by at least a decade of release. The 'Naughty Nineties' were the reaction to the horrors of the Crimea, the 'Roaring Twenties' followed the unbelievable hell of World War I and the 'Swinging Sixties' were induced by a combination of the Second World War and the privations inflicted by an inept and austere Labour Government between 1945 and 1951. A similar pattern is emerging in the former Soviet Russia today.

Inevitably the fifties were a fallow 'back to normal' period during which an unsuspecting populace went about their business reasonably confident that pre-war standards still prevailed, the proletariat would do what it was told and the stock markets would boom; as indeed they did in 1959, when Harold Macmillan observed that, 'We'd never had it so good.'

In fact this quote out of context, was a preliminary to a warning about taking too much for granted, but the phrase was too graphic for the media to ignore. However, in a north-western dockyard city where cosy middle-class conventions did not always apply, four mop-headed youths symbolised a change in the face of the nation which later forged attitudes still haunting society as I write. The perversely misspelt name said it all and Beatlemania took a generation by the throat.

For an organisation such as the Jockey Club, this was a tough act to follow. Essentially an upper-class institution, they found social levelling hard to grasp.

Accordingly they didn't bother and instead went about improving racing as they saw fit in a series of practical reports and decisions based on them.

This blinkered but understandable attitude had certainly contributed to the loss of a golden opportunity to put the financial future of the sport on a proper footing for ever with the advent of legalised off-course betting and ironically lack of money for racing became an increasing obsession.

The issues principally addressed at the time were those most likely to have an impact on the racegoer and punter; doping, starting stalls and the overnight declaration of jockeys. From the aspect of racing pure and simple, the Norfolk Committee's report on the Pattern of Racing was of paramount importance in shaping the future of the sport. The Club ostrich might have had its head in the sand financially and socially speaking, but racing was slowly accumulating long term benefits.

The idea of starting stalls for flat races had long burned in the racegoing public's mind. The art of starting, as practised by senior jockeys over the years, was a joy to behold and the likes of Richards, Smirke, Harry Wragg and the Smith brothers were rarely caught flat-footed, especially in sprints. They exercised a skill founded on horsemanship, one-upmanship, anticipation combined with elementary mind reading, and not a little intimidation of their opponents and sometimes officials.

The heirs and successors to such riders, the Piggotts, Carsons, Mercers and Cooks, were equally expert at gaining such legitimate advantage, but by the mid-sixties, the off-course punter paying the betting levy and wallowing in the new awareness brought about by betting shop sound commentaries, demanded something more akin to a fair start. Certainly, the start of maiden races with large fields, with many of the animals facing the five string barrier for the first time, flapping and grinding as it shot to the top of the starting post on release, was not a happy sight and more than one two-year-old was mentally scarred, and scared, for life.

Accordingly, starting stalls were first introduced at Newmarket on 8th July, 1965 and became a permanent feature in 1967. Finance was initially the responsibility of the Jockey Club, but eventually taken over by Racecourse Technical Services, founded by the Levy Board.

The cost was estimated at £170 per day for 135 days racing on 28 courses from Ayr to Brighton. Newmarket had the lion's share with 16 days, but Newbury did well with 11 and Ascot, naturally enough, took 15, while Wolverhampton racegoers experienced the novelty of mechanical starting for 1 day only on 12th June.

The system cannot be ideal and was not encouraged by the late Duke of Norfolk when he was Senior Steward. He was not the only one to have misgivings; some horses are simply too big for the traps and develop a phobia, others are reluctant to enter and delay races for many minutes, while the art of jockeyship has lost a dimension only realised by the modern racegoer when sprints such as the Portland Handicap at Doncaster in 1986 had to be started by flag, if ground conditions prohibit the weight of the stalls. The ensuing shambles was of little use to owner, trainer, jockey or punter. Admittedly, stalls have produced their own brand of starting skills amongst the knights of the pigskin, but they can hardly be described as artistic.

Of greater importance than starting techniques was the ever present menace of doping, again only recognised when a spectacular case comes to light and much media coverage ensues.

Well, journalists are only human and doping fits the well-fostered image of racing in the days of Nat Gould and Edgar Wallace and Dick Francis in modern times; the 'Sport of Kings' – even if this was Surtees's description of foxhunting and not intended to apply to the Turf. There is a brittle atmosphere of cocktails, caviar and countesses on the one hand with crooked trainers, bent jockeys and the shady owners of dubious military rank escorting ladies of even more dubious reputation, on the other.

Following a well publicised case with the innocent involvement of Sir Gordon Richards, the Jockey Club appointed a committee chaired by the late Duke of Norfolk in 1960 to enquire into the doping of racehorses, including those running under the Rules of the National Hunt Committee.

The Duke of Norfolk in the Ascot royal party, 1956. Apart from serving as Steward of the Jockey Club and Vice-Chairman of the Turf Board, he headed the Norfolk Committee on the future of racing and another on doping and made many other valuable contributions to racing. Also with Scobie Breasley after winning the Gimcrack Stakes in 1961.

The report of the committee in May 1961 was comprehensive for the period and the recommendations so wide ranging that one wonders what degree of action was being taken before, especially in the field of security. Superficially it seems that little had been achieved since the time of George Lambton, who's words of 1903 ironically preface the report.

For instance, although it must be remembered that we are reading of a pre-motorway age, a feature of the report was the observance that horses were despatched by box for 'up to eighty miles in the day to race and return...', 'certain boxes always stopped at certain cafés for the drivers to have a rest and a meal. It is, or anyway it was, quite normal for locals to ask to see the horses and to make inquiries about them. We are not satisfied that trainers fully realise the danger at this particular hour when they themselves admit that they are nowhere near.'

From the trainers point of view, this breathtaking degree of laxity could be serious at the time when any horse found to be doped, either to win or lose, was considered to be the absolute responsibility of the trainer and there was only one punishment: warned off indefinitely. The same applied to the horse, which could never run again under Jockey Club Rules, or anywhere else in the world where the Rules were reciprocated.

Admittedly, the report takes cognisance of this, sympathising with the trainer in the execution of his duties and responsibilities and acknowledging that he could not be in several places at once while emphasising the reliance which the trainer must place on his senior staff. Rule changes were suggested to eliminate the automatic withdrawal of the trainer's licence if the stewards were satisfied that he was not party to the doping. (NB: There were no women trainers at this time.)

A key clause in the report, which is still relevant today, reads: 'From the evidence it would appear that doping to stop is more prevalent today. To say that a trainer dopes to stop is, in our belief, bordering on the ridiculous. Any trainer has plenty of other ways of stopping a horse. But if an outside man can nobble favourites he runs no risk when he lays it. It must be the surest and safest bet.'

Indeed it is. The report goes on to make various fairly obvious recommendations such as the timing of medication prior to a race to avoid misplaced accusations of doping however inadvertent and there is a welter of clinical and medical evidence but the emphasis, rightly, is on prevention and deterrents.

However, much reliance was put on routine, selective and surprise samplings, in the belief that these measures would deter the doper. Unless taken before a race, they clearly do not. Once a horse has won or lost bets are settled and it matters not to the nobbler to lose, or the hotter to win; the losers have lost and the winner may be disqualified if detected at an inquiry weeks or months ahead, but the money has changed hands.

The testing of every horse in every race is clearly impractical except in very small fields, and this is acknowledged in the report. This is still true today and it is also true that most depressants given to a horse must be administered between 160 to 60 minutes before the race, less the drug works too soon or too late and virtually rules out the possibility of dope being given in the animals home stable. This report avers, 'We wish to emphasise that we have received no evidence to suggest that security at racecourse stables is not completely satisfactory.'

With hindsight, of course, it could not have been, but it would be wrong and unfair to denigrate the Norfolk Report on the grounds of naïveté. A lot of important work was done, including the establishment of the Forensic Laboratory at Newmarket in 1962 and the base was laid for the much more sophisticated Joint Racing Board Report on the scheme for the suppression of doping chaired by Professor W D M Paton in 1971.

Having stated that they were as impressed by the efficiency of some feature of the existing scheme as they were taken aback by the deficiencies in others, the scope of the Paton papers made the Norfolk Committee's conclusions read like an end of term assessment of a pupil at the better class of preparatory school. It returns to the problem of pre-race testing and concludes, rightly that this is 'the only procedure which despite its difficulties could take the profit out of doping'. The report goes on to suggest that a 'ruling commitment should be made to introduce pre-race testing when it becomes technically and economically feasible'. As noted above, it never has been.

The timing of the report was extremely pertinent. In 1970, the growth of interest in the actions of drugs and chemicals on humans, on animals and the environment together with the rapid technological advances of recent years were opening up new possibilities of analysis and control.

On that side, ie the chemical and analytical, the committee was uncritical, but it was extremely disturbed by the delay in action when a positive doping was detected and before the inspector of security was empowered by the stewards to take action. This was because a positive found by the laboratory had to be confirmed by another analyst before anything could be done.

This literal bolting of the door after the horse had gone was confirmed in Paton with the words, 'It is an important part of any deterrent that wrongdoers realise that as soon as it is established a crime has been committed the security machinery, in co-operation with the local police force, swing into action... these changes must reflect complete confidence by the racing authorities in their own forensic laboratory.'

Thankfully, this was taken to heart and full confidence placed in the Newmarket Horseracing Forensic Laboratory – without such confidence, the Club could never have fought and won the now notorious Aliysa case brought by H H Aga Khan IV following the disqualification of his filly after the Oaks in 1989.

As a result the Aga, who had crossed swords with the authorities before over such matters, notably the Vayrann case in 1982, when he was given the benefit of the doubt after Vayrann had tested positive for steroids following his victory in the Champion Stakes in 1981, resigned from the Jockey Club.

Since then, the European Horserace Scientific Liaison Committee has been formed to co-ordinate action and analysis on prohibited substances encountered by the three participating countries: France, Great Britain and Ireland, with harmonisation of testing procedures the priority issue, essential in an era of increasing international racing.

The Aga Khan leading in his 1936 Derby winner Mahmoud. His grandson had a less happy experience when Aliysa was disqualified from the Oaks.

*Corner of the Birdcage,
Newmarket, where the
crowd are waiting for the
numbers to be posted on the
board for the next race —
pre overnight declaration.*

Corner of the Birdcage, Newmarket, where the crowd are waiting for the numbers to be posted on the board for the next race — pre overnight declaration.

The third punter-related reform was the introduction of overnight declaration of runners in 1960, which was followed three decades later by the overnight declaration of jockeys; the fine tuning included a similar pre-nocturnal notification of blinkers and the draw. These measures became essential once off-course betting became legal and bookmakers' shops flourished in every high street, and had been recommended by the Duke of Devonshire's committee in 1958 in anticipation of the 1960 Betting and Gaming Act.

In general, the old system had been of considerable advantage to the bookmakers with the punter having no dependable information as to which horse would run and which wouldn't. The cards were published in the sporting and daily newspapers with the separate heading 'probables' and 'also engaged'. The 'probables' were assessed by the Press Association reporters, together with likely riding arrangements, and 'Also Engaged' represented the remaining entrants, supposedly unlikely to run.

However they could and did, as in theory any entry could run, and the final list of runners, jockeys and draw was not known until forty-five minutes before the off-time and not hoisted into the number board on the course until about twenty minutes before the race. In practice, there were on average at least one and often two surprise runners from the 'also engaged' pack each day and the discrepancy between 'probables' and actual runners was as high as 22 per cent.

Apart from the off-course backer wagering either illegally in cash or within the law on credit, the prime sufferer was the Tote, which had to operate on course for each race at very short notice, at a loss estimated at £100,000 a year — and it was impossible to establish such money-spinning pools as the Jackpot and the Placepot.

Off-course the then Tote Investors were forced to void many bets on non-runners and each-way wagers as fields cut up. As the old system passed, one

Again at the Birdcage – inspecting runners before the Cesarewitch.

or two hardened punters felt a twinge of regret. It was the period of strictly honoured jockeys' retainers and a popular system was to name a leading rider at the meeting (say Doug Smith) who was not jocked up in the 'probables' but one of who's owners or trainers had an entry in the 'also engaged' list. My late father landed a few nice 'touches' with this method.

In terms of racing in most aspects there were three major reports brought to bear; the Howard Committee of 1964, the Norfolk Committee of 1965 and the Benson Committee in 1968.

Lord Howard de Walden – aesthete and sportsman and Senior Steward of the Jockey Club 1957 and 1964.

Lord Howard de Walden was in his second term as Senior Steward when he chaired the Howard Committee. It was a hard look at racing as it stood in the administrative sense and had an eye towards the reorganisation of that side, together with the inevitable considerations of the industrial scene.

There seemed no wish to dominate the racing industry; on the contrary, the Club had delegated power to, amongst others, the Racecourse Association which forced every racecourse to become a member, much to the disgust of Mrs Mirabel Topham. This formidable lady was then the owner of Aintree and racing's very own Mad Woman of Chaillot. It was not until Lord Howard had made it plain that he might have to incur the embarrassment of prohibiting the Grand National that the former chorus girl gave in.

On the other hand, it was clear that since the advent of the Levy Board, a new picture had emerged. Racing was financially in a bad way and the options were to give the board its head in leading the industry, or whether the Jockey Club and the National Hunt Committee should blend with the Board and run the show as an entity, industry and administration indivisibly linked.

It followed that the Club could not maintain the traditional role as administrators while allowing the Board to attain industrial control and propagating a 'tail wagging the dog' situation. Accordingly, the Howard report recommended an amalgamation of the Turf authorities, to be known as the Turf Board.

The new Board would incorporate representatives of the Levy Board and the courses, trainers, owners and breeders by way of an advisory council and of course the Jockey Club and National Hunt Committee would be represented. As an administrative body, the Board would have a director and a secretariat, thus reducing the responsibilities (and the £60,000 pa cost) of Weatherby's, although the latter organisation would continue to operate the Registry Office, act as Secretaries to both Jockey Club and the National Hunt Committee and profit from the various spin-offs, such as banking, printing and the publication of the *Stud Book* and the *Calendar*.

Newmarket, as Jockey Club Estates, would devolve from the Club's central operation and act as a subsidiary organisation supervised by the Jockey Club Agent, with the Clerk of the Course in a subordinate capacity.

CHAPTER 12

Money, Money, Money

When the Turf Board was set up on 1st January 1965, racing was still muddling through. This need not have been so. Had the racing lobby made a greater impact on the passage and provisions of the 1960 Betting and Gaming Act, the sport could have been on a financial footing which would have secured a substantial and adequate income from gambling for all time.

The legislation, by legalising betting shops or off-course cash wagering, was to lead the way to a charge for the benefit of racing levied on the bookmakers who had lived high on the hog from the sport for many years. The downside was that where a levy began, taxation of betting would not be far behind. Both came to pass.

It fell to two members of the Astor family to pave the route on behalf of the Turf: The Hon. John (later Sir John) Astor in the Commons between 1951 and 1959 and his brother Viscount Astor in the Lords. The Duke of Norfolk was also to the fore. The Royal Commission on Betting, Lotteries and Gaming had reported in 1951 that the ludicrous anomalies of off-course and on-course betting should be removed and the Government decided to act upon the findings.

At first, John Astor thought that a Tote monopoly could be achieved. The bookmakers had done well enough and the Tote had a decent record of serving the sport over two decades, albeit with a miserable market share. It is breathtaking to think what might have happened if a Tote monopoly had been set up in 1960 or 1961, with outlets in every High Street as well as on-course. The political reality and the weight of the bookmakers' money ensured that this Utopian dream was never realised.

The Duke of Norfolk, who retired as Senior Steward in 1955, asked the Chancellor of the Exchequer to reduce the rate of tax on the Tote, then running at 47 per cent, and to remove the stupid Entertainment Tax on gate money. This imposition was intended primarily to raise revenue from the cinematic and theatrical industries and like the Selective Employment Tax in the sixties, none the better for that.

Entertainment Tax was abolished in 1957. Norfolk thought that the planned legislation might provide the opportunity for a levy on bookmakers as an interim measure, but hoped for abolition of the leggers in the long term.

Some hope. The bookmakers were admittedly in a state of anxiety, but were sensible enough to realise that paying a levy was better than abolition, although they jibbed at the idea of legalised off-course betting. They were afraid of taxation on legal wagers, petty restrictions effecting the operation of betting shops and of course they loathed the thought of the obvious, the introduction of a Tote monopoly. In other words, they preferred non-taxable illegality to taxed respectability and their duty as responsible citizens.

Al Capone and Legs Diamond doubtless feared the repeal of Prohibition for similar reasons, and when it came to the inevitable legislation the bookies brought all their street-wise forces to bear.

John Astor's original hope for a Tote monopoly had evaporated by 1956, principally because the Jockey Club did not support the idea, on the grounds that there was little enthusiasm from the racegoers or the public at large.

The story began in the Commons on 9th March 1956, following a debate in the Lords on 8th February when Lord Silkin drew attention to the fact that the report of the 1951 Royal Commission was still gathering dust, despite promises of action by the administration. The Government made the usual excuse of lack of Parliamentary time but, prodded into stirring their stumps, debates on the report took place in both Houses.

Those who took part in the Commons debate instigated by Arthur Lewis, apart from Astor, who concluded his speech in true sporting style with the declaration, 'I would rather win the Derby than an election' (eventually he had to settle for the St Leger with Provoke in 1965) included George Wigg, of whom much more later. Wigg stated that he did not think any government would do anything about betting generally although he thought it ought to tackle the problem of street betting. This half-cock proposal was followed by a fierce criticism of the Jockey Club, which he described as 'a terrible organisation'.

W.F. (later Lord) Deedes, Joint Under-Secretary of State at the Home Office, said that his department agreed with the report insofar as the current legal position was not satisfactory; the Government were in favour of off-course betting parlours, adding the usual rider of the difficulty of finding time for a bill in the crowded Commons timetable.

This was interpreted as a declaration of intent, and the Home Office contacted the Chairman of the Bookmakers' Executive Committee to ask for a deputation to visit the Under-Secretary and discuss the proposed legislation. The bookmakers complied, commenting that, 'The situation was now very grave for them.'

The first major speech on the issue was by Viscount Astor in the Lords on 25th June 1956. His statement was well prepared and thoroughly researched. He emphasised the need for some income for racing from betting and he stat-

ed the case again for a Tote monopoly on the French and American models. Pursuing the arguments for 'clean-up' legislation, he castigated the bookmakers, whose illegal off-course activities corrupted the police and it was clear that the 'laundered' betting profits could finance other crimes as well. Astor mitigated his remarks when adding that there were doubtless, 'many fine respectable honest bookmakers', although he went on, 'but the present system makes a border-line between betting and crime which I am sure the police and all interested in law and order, would be delighted to see finished once and for all by the establishment of the same totalisator monopoly in this country as has proved successful in our main competitors.'

Richard 'Dick' Dunn's powerful voice could be heard along most racecourse rails – but especially Hurst Park. A contemporary writer noted "He who saw Dick Dunn in the Ring for the first time would probably marvel at the beauty and sparkle of his diamonds". Also look at the smart dress of 'Sobersides' his clerk.

Realistically conceding that the Tote monopoly idea would fail, Lord Astor went on to urge the licensing and control of off-course bookmakers and put forward a detailed argument for a levy on book-makers' turnover, on and off-course, citing the already successful system operating in Ireland. While advocating a greater freedom for the Tote, he mentioned as a tailpiece, '... a sinister alliance between the Church Committee on Betting and bookmakers to oppose the betting shops... the Church Committee think that to have betting shops would encourage betting and make it too respectable. The bookmakers seem to prefer the present system, where they are without control, without licence and taxation....'

Well, as the lady said in court, they would, wouldn't they? As has been pointed out in previous chapters, no government can tax illegal transactions and thus the bookmakers be compelled to pay anything towards the upkeep of the creature on which the parasites depended.

Lord Astor's speech was a benchmark; widely reported, it cleared the air and the public now knew what racing and breeding needed to continue to provide them with their entertainment on a reasonable scale.

At this point H H Aga Khan III decided to enter the fray via a letter to *The Times* calling for a Tote monopoly and complaining that the economics of the British Turf forced owners to sell their best stock to the USA. Lord Rosebery, justifiably irritated by this prime example of the pot calling the kettle black, replied in the same correspondence column that the Aga was the worst offender, having sold all four of his Derby winners to American breeders. Touché; and Rosebery might have added that the Aga's attitude was not so evident when he bought his way into racing in the twenties, when circumstances were exactly the same.

Despite Lord Astor's speech, legislation remained in the doldrums. A major difficulty was that the 1951 Royal Commission made no recommendations as to a levy, which the Government found useful as yet another excuse to delay matters.

In this uncertain atmosphere, various attempts were made at what might be called mini-legislation. In 1957 George Wigg offered a Betting Reform Bill which would have extended the powers of the Racecourse Betting Control Board which ran the Tote. The Bill would have denied the right of the bookmakers to take bets at Tote odds, while the Tote could accept cash bets by post and permit callers at Tote offices to bet on credit. The bookmakers' lobby went into action with the justification that the Royal Commission had discouraged piecemeal legislation and the Bill failed at its Second Reading.

Another Bill with similar objectives introduced by Sir Eric Errington in 1959 was better drafted but met the same fate at the tender hands of the bookmakers 'friends' in Parliament led by Stephen (later Sir Stephen) McAdden. It must be remembered in this context that in those days there was no register of MP's interests outside Parliament, as declared by the Member. The possibilities for what is now known as 'sleaze' were unlimited, and the bookmakers were fighting for their lives on their own admission. Of course Members of Parliament are honourable and describe themselves as such in debate, but while there may be no such thing as a free lunch, there certainly is such a thing as a free bet.

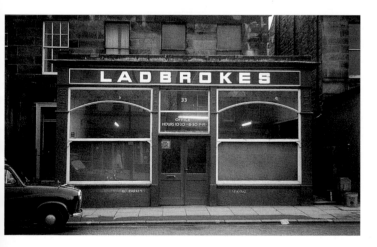 

Ladbroke's first and one of their latest betting shops – Raeburn Place and Porland Road, Hove, Sussex.

These Parliamentary reverses should have alerted the Jockey Club to the rocks ahead; but either through an over-developed sense of right, justice and fairness or innocent blinkered thinking, this did not happen.

Rather, Daniel entered the lions' den and in the *Calendar* of 6th May 1956, announced the formation of the Joint Betting Bill Committee, chaired by the Senior Steward, Lord Willoughby de Broke. Members were drawn from the Jockey Club and the National Hunt Committee, together with delegates from

The idea of an 'owners strike' which included the Queen and Queen Mother on the issue of bookies paying up.

the Racecourse Betting Control Board, Tote Investors, the Thoroughbred Breeders' Association, the Racecourse Association, Tattersalls Committee, the Racehorse Owner's Association and representatives of the bookmakers and the press. The declared objective was to agree the principles on which the proposed legislation should be based.

The bookies were not giving much away. They were happy to negotiate on any payments which they were forced to make for licences or registration but they did not want registration to be handled by the Racecourse Betting Control Board and in effect wished to licence themselves if this were not done by a court of law. They remained opposed to betting shops and preferred that the Street Betting Act of 1906 should be repealed; ie street betting should be legal but remain uncontrolled with no benefit to racing.

Astonishingly, the Betting Bill Committee agreed to these proposals with the exception of the latter. The Stewards were invited to put to the Home Secretary, Major Gwylm Lloyd George, the case for betting supporting racing. Unfortunately, Lloyd George was not able to find a formula which appealed to the Stewards. The Club seemed determined, in spite of this set-back, not to promote a lobby on behalf of the Turf in Parliament, but to rely on the Betting Committee, excluding the other potential allies and depending on the Stewards' 'close touch' with Government ministers'. Since the bookmakers appeared to dominate the Committee, the 'old boy' network was a feeble substitute for an all-out Parliamentary campaign.

This approach was to cost racing dearly when the chips were down for the Betting and Gaming Act of 1960, as the then Home Secretary, R A Butler, was never given a proper idea of the needs of racing. Nonetheless, the wheeling and dealing continued and at one point the Home Office offered the Jockey Club a package which provided for a partial Tote monopoly including cash betting shops with off-course bookmakers limited to credit and cash-by-post transactions, but there would be no levy.

Wisely, the Club rejected this proposal and insisted that all betting on racing should contribute to the sport. The bookmakers were not enthralled with the idea either; although it killed the bogey of a levy, it smacked too much of a Tote monopoly via the back door.

Meanwhile, some racecourse executives were thinking up ploys to raise money from the on-course bookmakers. The Racecourse Association demanded from the Exchange Telegraph Company, otherwise known as Extel, about £2,000,000 to be collected from bookmakers as a surcharge for the use of Extel's telephone which 'blew' money from the course to off-course and vice-versa, plus a commentary on the races.

Mrs Mirabel Topham on behalf of Aintree and formidable as ever, confused the picture as she inevitably would by requesting an increase in the rental of Extel phones from £240 per annum to £5,000. Neither schemes came to fruition, and in any case the Jockey Club rightly disapproved. The relieved bookmakers continued their negotiations with the Club on the wider issue of a controlled levy which they now accepted was their best chance of survival.

At this stage, the Bookmakers' Committee discussed the improbable idea of the Royal Charter, thus providing the option of a body which would have sufficient status to raise a levy independently of any statutory organisation imposed by Government.

The bookmakers were advised that it was unlikely that the Privy Council would approve a Royal Charter and it was mooted that a Private Member's Bill should be drafted. This would have little chance of success, but at least establish the layers' point of view. The main point was that the bookmakers would register members of the profession and have the power to raise a levy from them, and unregistered bookies could not operate legally.

In the interim, they had approached the Stewards with a scheme of a voluntary fund raising approximately £100,000 if the idea was supported by the Jockey Club. The fund, to be called either The Stewards' Fund or The Racecourse Improvement Fund, was intended primarily to improve amenities on racetracks and a quid pro quo to persuade the Club to get the RCA off the bookies' backs.

Well, we would all like to determine our own rate of taxation, but in any case time was running out. On 3rd July 1959 the Home Office informed all parties that submissions regarding betting legislation had to be in hand, and the matter closed by the time the Commons went into recess on 30th July. As the Jockey Club had already submitted the final scheme which put the registration of bookmakers and the collection of a levy in the power of the Racecourse Betting Control Board, a situation completely and understandably unacceptable to the bookies; and notwithstanding the contents of their draft Bill, the leggers had to act fast.

On 16th July they met with the Stewards at Newmarket and were informed by E W Weatherby, representing the Jockey Club's long serving secretariat, that the Home Office had suggested the Stewards' plan should be modified to the extent that bookmakers would be licenced by the Government, but under the jurisdiction of the Government body of three, which would oversee two boards: one a variation of the Racecourse Betting Control Board in charge of the Tote and the other a board of bookmakers answerable for the regulation of their fellows. These boards could levy money for the benefit of racing, should the Racecourse Amenities Fund prove to be inadequate (which it was; only £45,000 was raised for racecourses in 1959).

This was the best deal the bookies had scented so far, and it was the time to talk turkey. The Jockey Club reckoned that racing needed £3,000,000 a year from betting revenue. The layers, naturally enough, thought the sum too high, 'and it would be better to start lower and work up'. The vital question of who was to be empowered to spend the funds arising from a levy remained unresolved, although the bookmakers wanted as much authority as could be marshalled.

The Betting and Gaming Bill was announced in the Queen's Speech on 27th October 1959, presented to the House three days later by R A Butler and given its First Reading. However, there was no provision in the Bill for a statutory levy on betting for the benefit of racing, although the principle of a levy was by now so firmly established that it should have been incorporated. Most betting, legal or illegal, was on racing and it was a costly moment for the Club to be brushed aside by Butler on 2nd November, shortly after the First Reading, when he replied to a written question in the Commons:

> The Stewards of the Jockey Club and other bodies concerned with the sport of horseracing and the breeding of racehorses, have made representations to me that any Bill relating to betting should include provision for a compulsory levy on off-the-course betting on horseraces, the proceeds to be devoted, like the surplus from the Totalisator, to the support of horseracing and breeding. This proposal was not considered by the Royal Commission on Betting, Lotteries and Gaming 1949–52; it raises important issues of principle and presents serious practical difficulties.

Certainly, but this should have come as no great surprise to Butler, to Parliament or to the civil servants; after all the matter had been debated in both houses and submissions to the Home Office made for the best part of a decade. As it was, racing got fobbed off by the appointment of Sir Leslie Peppiatt to chair a committee to 'consider the desirability and practicability of bookmakers contributing to racing and breeding and if they favoured it to advise on its amount and how it should be raised'.

Of course, the main thrust of the Bill was to tidy up Britain's archaic gambling laws, some of which had laid untouched for over a hundred years. The

Bill achieved its purpose and although an over-anxiety to please churchmen and not to be seen to encourage people to bet resulted in betting shops ending up, in the words of R A Butler, 'more like undertakers premises'.

Subsequent legislation to allow evening opening, television and clear-glass windows, plus coffee machines, carpets and other facilities for the punter have done much to erode the old 'spit and sawdust' image. Contrary to the bookies' original fears, betting shops have proved to be extremely profitable, as the accounts of Hills, Corals and Ladbrokes will testify.

Quite reasonably, the Jockey Club had insisted that bookmakers should be registered by the Racecourse Betting Control Board, which would collect a levy. The bookmakers, naturally enough, wanted to run their own ship and apparently be responsible to no-one. The compromise of a statutory body was a fine get-out for Butler and his 'Sir Humphreys', but racing was to be the loser.

Put bluntly, the Jockey Club needed to regulate the bookmakers and collect and distribute the monies to which racing had a legitimate claim. Even the layers recognised this while the bookmakers thought they could regulate themselves although they had operated illegally and made illicit profits for generations, corrupting law enforcement officers and Lord knows who else in the process. On the other hand, the Club had ruled a high money sport for two centuries with a degree of integrity which was the envy of the sporting world. It is obvious who should have prevailed, but the bookies' 'greased palm' philosophy won the day.

Not surprisingly, the Peppiatt Committee decided that a levy would be a good thing. Reporting in April 1960 they concluded, 'that a levy is required... the infusion of fresh money should be regarded not as serving to bolster a declining industry but as an aid to improving it'.

Then came the question of how much? The Committee knew the current figures: £450,000 from the charges to ply their trade on the racetracks, and £685,000 from the Racecourse Betting Control Board, a total of £1,135,000. The Jockey Club's request for £3,000,000 stood. The bookmakers reckoned that a levy would provide £1,250,000 in its first year. Peppiatt meekly accepted this and the resulting shortfall of £400,000.

Unhappily, this was to be the pattern for some years to come. The bookies were in the box seat, cheerfully quoting the usual clichés about 'capacity to pay'. However, the layers assertion that 87 per cent of all bookmakers grossed less than £3,000 p.a. was greeted with some scepticism by Parliament, especially as in Ireland the yield for their 1958 levy was £1,024,000 based on a turnover of a mere £14,684,000 and Ireland even then enjoyed far fewer race days. Would that the British levy were to be based on turnover; instead it was initially based on that boon to 'creative' accounting, net profit.

George Wigg saw through this stupidity, and waxed angry with the bookmakers. During the Third Reading of the Betting Levy Bill on 20th December 1960, he commented to Stephen McAdden, the bookies' friend, 'I would remind him (McAdden) of some of the things that are being said in the pubs and clubs at present. They are very unpleasant. It is suggested that the Government have given increased pay to the police as a quid pro quo for the bribes that they will not now get from bookmakers. I do not associate myself with that.'

On this occasion, Wigg's latterly notorious pluralism was on the side of the Jockey Club, or at least racing which he genuinely loved. It fell to Chuter Ede, a former Home Secretary, to push the dagger of socialist hypocrisy into the side of the Jockey Club: 'Who would have thought,' he declared as the Bill was passed, '... that we should see the Stewards of the Jockey Club and people interested in horse breeding in this House watching the passing of a measure which would transfer from the pockets of the proletariat money which would go to the upkeep of their sport and the racecourses and breeding in which they take such a delight. This indeed is the most curious but the most striking example of the way in which we now all accept the benefits of the Welfare State.'

The Farewell State some of us called it at the time, and we may yet be proved right. In any case we all pay taxes, even Jockey Club members who may well pay more than most, and it seems an odd principle that any taxpayer should be denied State benefits just because they are racehorse owners and breeders, albeit members of the Jockey Club.

Also the levy was on the bookmakers and they had no justification then, and none now, for passing on the cost to the public, although this had been anticipated by the Peppiatt Committee. Having decided that the levy should be on bookmakers rather than on backers, the report observed with a well-founded cynicism, 'We are not at all convinced that in the end means would not be found to pass on at least part of it directly or indirectly...'.

The Betting Levy Bill became law on 28th March 1961, and was effective as from 1st September. The Levy Board consisted of two delegates from the Jockey Club, one from the National Hunt Committee, the Chairman of the Tote and the Bookmakers' Committee were ex-officio members plus three Home Office mandarins, officially and rather intriguingly described as 'persons who have no interests connected with horseracing which might hinder them from discharging their functions in an impartial manner'. This was because their duties included arbitrating in disputes over the amount of the levy.

The Chairman was Field Marshal Lord Harding of Petherton, a distinguished soldier who had won the DSO and two bars. Harding completed his military service as Chief of the Imperial General Staff; a former amateur rider, he also enjoyed polo and pig-sticking in quite the right way when serving in India between the wars.

The new Board virtually took over the former Racecourse Betting Control Board, which in turn became the Totalisator Board, in charge of pool betting with an obligatory annual contribution to the levy. Originally, assessment was based on the number of shops operated by the bookmaker and a charge on net profits. In 1968 this was replaced by a partial levy on turnover, whilst some charge on profits was maintained. Eventually, five years later, the levy was simply based on turnover, which it should have been in the first place.

Harding was a good chairman, who was at ease with the Jockey Club. The only difference was the usual question, still alive today, as to who was to spend the levy yield. The Club still thought that this was their responsibility, as the cash was collected by the Board in the name or racing, which the Club controlled. Harding demurred and the Jockey Club did not, at this stage, press the point.

In any case, Harding's Board could not be said to have served racing badly in the matter of expenditure. Essential operations such as Racecourse Technical Services, which provided the photo-finish, camera patrol, starting stalls, stable security, anti-doping measures and even the cost of overnight declarations, all benefited from the levy, as did prize money.

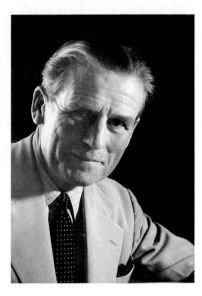

Lord Harding.

In 1963, £69,000 went to top-class races and £227,228 to help the lesser lights running in minimum value races. In the same year, the Board took control of the National Stud. This was achieved in spite of a pathetic first year income of only £892,617, against the bookmakers own estimate of £1,250,000 and a shortfall of £2,107,383 on the Jockey Club's £3,000,000 estimate of need.

Although the Levy Board by now agreed that even this figure was too low, it was also too late. Before the levy became based solely on turnover in 1973, it never exceeded around £2,000,000 but by 1974 was providing £6,659,145.

This figure was reached under the chairmanship of Colonel George (later Lord) Wigg. Harding and Wigg were soldiers who had served their country well and both were graduates of Grammar Schools. The urbane Field Marshal and the former Colonel in the Education Corps also shared a love of racing and the army, but in social attitudes they were poles apart. Wigg had risen through the ranks and in 1945 was elected MP for Dudley. His Commons career was distinguished, serving as Parliamentary Private Secretary to Emmanuel Shinwell when the latter was in turn Minister of Fuel, Secretary of State for War and Minister of Defence. Given Shinwell's views on racing as recorded in Chapter Ten, presumably the Turf was a taboo subject between them.

Always a man with his ear to the ground, Wigg played a leading part in uncovering the Profumo scandal and later served in the nominal guise of Paymaster General as Harold (now Lord) Wilson's security 'watchdog' during Wilson's premiership. This liaison was hardly surprising, since both men possessed acute minds which made Niccolo ('the end justifies the means') Machiavelli seem as naive as the author of 'Scouting for Boys'.

Wigg became a member of the Racecourse Betting Control Board in 1958

George Wigg.

and continued to serve when that body became the Tote Board, until 1964. In 1967 Wigg quit politics was elevated to the peerage and became Chairman of the Levy Board.

Things did not get off to a happy start in respect of Lord Wigg's relationship with the Jockey Club. The Turf Board invited him to Portman Square where the Senior Steward, Major General Sir Randle Feilden, returned to the theme of responsibility for the expenditure of the Levy, a bone of contention which had laid dormant during the Harding years.

Feilden told Wigg that the Levy Board would collect and the Club spend. The Duke of Norfolk chipped in to instruct Wigg that he must never talk to the press on Turf matters without clearance from the Club.

Given Lord Wigg's independence of mind and ingrained social attitudes, his response was both predictable and justifiable. Employing some choice parade ground language, he told the Stewards that he was not in their thrall, and if they wished to consult him again he could be found at the Levy Board's office in Southampton Row.

This confrontation was clearly going to present some problems in the future and, to ease the situation, the Joint Racing Board was formed in April 1968 as a policy- making body under the joint chairmanship of the Senior Steward and the Chairman of the Levy Board. The other members were the Deputy Senior Steward, one other Jockey Club Steward and two of the Government appointees to the Levy Board.

If Wigg's relationship with the Jockey Club was prickly, his dealings with the bookmakers were also on some occasions far from cordial. Essentially a politician, Wigg was more popular with the mandarins of Whitehall than with the racing fraternity with whom he was supposed to be dealing. One measure which did not please the Home Office, however, was Wigg's 1969 amendment to the Horserace Betting Levy Act, which made the Home Secretary responsible for resolving disputed Levy Schemes, in place of the three Home Office appointees on the Board.

George Wigg's main difficulty was enforcing a scheme of payments based on bookmakers' turnover, although the principle had been agreed by all parties in 1967. Despite this, not all the layers were happy, especially the large firms who would obviously pay the most. There were several arguments over the seventh and eighth Levy Schemes, with 'capacity to pay' again rearing its irrelevant head. A fierce fight in the Commons went against the bookmakers and Lord Wigg got his way.

At long last, the Levy was on a proper basis. As the *Guardian* tartly pointed out, 'the Levy has been changed to one on turnover rather than profit because of the difficulty of finding out what profits a bookmaker makes. The point is that if he has not the capacity to pay, should he be allowed to continue in business?'

Precisely. At last that hollow argument was laid to rest and as the bookies feared, where the Levy went, betting tax was soon to follow, despite the by now well worn protests from the leggers about taxation driving betting underground, a subject on which the bookmakers had over half a century of experience. Also, they seemed to forget that it takes two to strike a bet, but they are well aware of this when refusing wagers if the stakes don't suit them.

A tax was introduced by way of the Budget in 1966 and was implemented in October of that year at a rate of 2.5 per cent, increased to 5 per cent in 1968 and at one point reached 8 per cent. In 1987, Betting Duty on-course was abolished to encourage racecourse attendances and is currently 7.75 per cent on off-course wagers.

There can be little doubt that the tax is a disincentive to bet and reductions can only help, albeit indirectly. Unlike the levy, it is a conventional indirect tax on the transaction and both bookmaker and punter are liable. In practice, the bookmaker acts as collector, either by way of the punter paying 'tax on', ie a percentage of his stake, or paying the same percentage as a deduction from any winnings. The bookmakers 'round up' this deduction to ten pence in the pound, comprising levy and tax totalling 8.75 per cent, the balance covering VAT and such sundries as lavatory paper in the staff loos – although quite why the punter has to pay for this relief is hard to fathom.

As Benjamin Franklin wryly observed, 'In this world nothing can be certain except death and taxes.' It is comforting to know that even the 'old enemy' laying the odds eventually grasped this simple truth.

CHAPTER 13

Wiggs on the Green

Wigg finally made his peace with the bookies, and the Levy Board acquired a degree of stability which was to continue under successive chairmen: Sir Stanley Raymond (1972/73), Sir Desmond Plummer, later Lord Plummer (1973/82) and Sir Ian Trethowan (1982/88). The present Chairman is Sir John Sparrow.

But the financial battles were far from over. By 1968 the Tote was running into difficulties. The machine now had two roles: the conventional on-course cash and off-course credit service based on the pool, and off-course betting outlets. The Tote's payments to the Levy Board were based on 1 and a half per cent of turnover for the former and paid the same rate as the bookmakers for the latter.

However, betting duty was increased from 2 and a half per cent to 5 per cent in March 1968, and the racing industry had yet to face up to the invidious Selective Employment Tax, a serious matter for the labour-intensive Tote. Furthermore, the 1969 Budget proposed a duty of three times the rateable value on all off-course betting premises. Already the Tote's contribution to the Levy was a mere £677,388, while the Government were collecting £922,832 in duty.

To meet these costs, deductions from losing stakes would have to be increased to 23 and a half per cent on win, place and forecast pools, and 25 per cent on the Jackpot, Daily Double and Treble. These increases were based on the level of 20 per cent imposed when Betting Duty came in at 2 and a half per cent in 1966.

At that time Wigg was still Paymaster General and attempted to intervene on the Tote's behalf but was blandly brushed aside by Roy Jenkins, later Lord Jenkins, then Home Secretary.

Things could only get worse and they did, in common with the deleterious state of the nation. Only £412,933 was raised for racing in 1970. The duty on premises was repealed, but betting tax rose to 6 per cent off-course while static at 5 per cent on-course.

The Tote was now effectively broke insofar as it could not pay its Levy contributions and owed £864,295. Although sympathetic, Wigg also had a duty to racing and the Board. He informed the Home Secretary that either that Minister should make a decision or the Board would have to seek a remedy through the courts, thus resulting in the unhappy spectacle of one statutory body suing another.

The Home Secretary's decision was that the Tote should pay nothing for 1970-71, presumably on the basis that it was broke and had no 'capacity' to pay. Wigg considered that the Tote should make a reasonable profit if it were efficiently run, and insisted on a 1 and a half per cent levy, arguing that the demand would help the Tote in obtaining legislation which would put it on a proper commercial footing.

On the other hand such reform was bound to be opposed by the bookmakers if it threatened their profits or trampled on their territory, as any improvement in the Tote's performance would surely do; the simple way for Goliath to have defeated David would have been to sabotage the latter's supply of stones.

Bookmakers no longer lived in the shadow of illegality as they had when the 1960 Act was being negotiated and they had gained bitter experience in 1979. A Bill to give the Tote the opportunity to 'compete fairly' with the bookmakers was given a First Reading in November 1971. The increase in betting off-course following the 1960 Act had left the Tote behind while the demands of the Levy had produced a crippling effect. Now, the Tote would be empowered to bet at fixed odds on any event except horse racing, which would be confined to pool betting. The joker in the pack was Clause 3 of the Bill; it would enable the Tote to set up in business on the high street without proving 'local demand', although this would require a little diplomacy to assuage local licensing J.P.s; the Government could, of course, provide this by way of an amendment at the Committee stage.

The layers went into battle with all guns blazing. A Bookmakers' Action Committee was formed, the Chairman of Ladbrokes, Cyril Stein, reputedly underwrote £100,000 of expenses to fight the Bill, while Brian Walden, the MP for a Birmingham constituency and later TV interviewer, was retained at a fee of £3,000 pa to act as Parliamentary adviser.

The bookie's delegates involved in the lobbying were accommodated at the Dorchester hotel, which slightly disconcerted Richard Burton, and lunches were arranged for groups of MPs: the Mirabelle restaurant for conservatives at £7 per head, and the Hyde Park hotel at £4 for the socialists (which I must say the author would have preferred). To round off, two receptions were staged at the Commons immediately prior to the Second Reading on 3rd February 1972.

Meanwhile, George Wigg had been having second thoughts. On 20th March he stated that it would be wrong to allow the Tote to enter bookmaking (on the grounds of incompetence) and equally wrong to permit the

'Nanny' to write off its debt to the Levy Board.

This volte-face did nothing to help the Bill's chances, and eventually only an emasculated version received the Royal Assent, with Clause 3 subject to a Commencement Order which was never sought. The Tote were now free to act as S.P. bookmakers, a move supported by the Jockey Club. Actually nothing had been gained.

Lord Wigg remained in office at the Levy Board until 1972, and in 1973 the gamekeeper turned poacher when he became Chairman of the Betting Office Licensees' Association, better known as B.O.L.A. Because of his political omnipotence at this time as far as racing affairs were concerned, Sir David Llewellyn, writing as 'Jack Logan' in the *Sporting Life*, described Wigg in a parody of the words of Andrew Lang, who himself was imitating Waldo Emerson:

I am the batsman and the bat,
I am the BOLA and the ball,
The umpire, the pavillion cat,
The roller, pitch and stumps and all.

Wigg's relationship with the Jockey Club eventually deteriorated to the point where the Duke of Norfolk, then Her Majesty's Representative, publicly and in the presence of HM Queen Elizabeth the Queen Mother, harangued Wigg for ten minutes over the public address system at an Ascot meeting.

Ostensibly, this was a reaction to the 1969 Gimcrack speech by David (later Sir David) Robinson, who said that racing should be run as a business and the Jockey Club had failed the sport financially. Robinson, a millionaire philanthropist who had made his fortune from renting radio and television sets, had just bought Kempton Park, which he intended to run as a successful business (he didn't achieve this eventually as he was denied the planning consents to develop the course), but Wigg picked up the sentiments of the Gimcrack speech and chucked in his own tuppence worth by referring to the Jockey Club as 'a well-kept veteran motor car, interesting for use on the occasional drive if you have infinite time and patience and willingness to judge the article by its original quality and value'.

Wigg exonerated the Stewards from this comparison, but matters were not assisted when it became known that the motoring allusion was the work of Lord Goodman, Harold Wilson's legal guru. Goodman often seemed to be sitting in front of more pies than he had fingers to insert in them and the plot literally thickened when it was revealed that the text had been approved by the Senior Steward, Sir Randle Feilden.

However, the Duke of Norfolk was oblivious of the authorship when he said at Ascot, 'He (Wigg) referred to the Stewards as being superb. He referred to the rest of the Jockey Club as being a veteran car. I have been a member of the Jockey Club for 36 years, and I served as a Steward for 15. Therefore in the eyes of Lord Wigg I have been superb for 15 years and now I belong to that car.'

Wigg was furious, not only because the racegoers applauded the Duke generously, but in his sometimes small-minded way he resented the fact that the Levy Board had paid for the public address system over which Norfolk had spoken!

Nonetheless, Wigg did much for racing, even if his class prejudice made it difficult for him to assist the real administration of the sport as he always seemed to be negative in that respect. In his days at the Levy Board he put racing's finances on a reasonable if inadequate footing but his finest achievement was the acquisition of Epsom, Sandown and Kempton for United Racecourses. Later these tracks passed into the control of Racecourse Holdings Trust and, thanks to Lord Wigg, such superb races as the Oaks, the Coronation Cup, the Eclipse Stakes, the King George VI Steeplechase and the Derby will be *ours* forever.

He established Racecourse Security Services, and pioneered the 'criteria' fixture list which guaranteed at least two meetings a day to keep the tills ringing in the betting shops.

Appropriately, a bust of Lord Wigg in bronze has a place of honour in the paddock at Epsom. There is a second bronze in the National Horseracing Museum at Newmarket which gazes thoughtfully at a portrait of his former adversary, Sir Randle Feilden. Old soldiers never die.

Geoffrey Freer, the Jockey Club's Senior handicapper from 1945-62, here at York races with Johnny Hislop (right). Freer's uncle T.F. Dawkins held the same post from 1912 to 1931.

It would have been easy enough for the Jockey Club to get bogged down in the politicking of the sixties and seventies, but in fact much was done as the Club quietly got on with the job of running racing.

It cannot be over-emphasised that all good racing stems from the top, a point well made in the report of the Duke of Norfolk's Committee on the Pattern of Racing. Convened in 1965, the members in addition to the Duke were Geoffrey Freer, the Senior Jockey Club handicapper and distinguished Clerk of several courses, plus Peter Willett, a leading authority on breeding.

Thirty years on, it is interesting to reflect on their recommendations. The committee concluded that there was too much prize money being allocated to precocious two-year-olds, and that large stakes were given for one or two races towards the end of the year which were not to be encouraged. A fair analysis might be that there was a preponderance of indiscriminate juvenile races, and that the 'championship' races culminating the season over five, six and seven furlongs might be the Cornwallis at Ascot, the Middle Park and the Dewhurst at Newmarket.

Believing that two-year-old races over a mile are not necessarily bad for the animal that is bred to stay but may prove harmful to the purely sprint-bred horse, the committee concluded that any juvenile race for high stakes should be run over a round course. Overall, the two-year-old season was unevenly spread and encouraged the unscrupulous owner or trainer to hurry a young animal.

Today the chickens have come home to roost for the exploiters of the 'early sort' of two-year-old. The programme for Competitive Racing, issued in 1993 by a development group headed by David Oldrey, diminished open maidens from 336 to 240. There were howls of anguish, but anyone with the welfare of the thoroughbred at heart would have to agree with this measure, albeit introduced a little late in the day.

Theoretically, the 'Pattern' or classic horse is spared the indignity of exploitation, but as the weakness of the breed has become more evident in recent seasons, the wisdom of racing juveniles over distances in excess of seven furlongs or a mile must be questioned.

Moving on to three-year-olds, the committee acknowledged that they were well catered for, but this was very largely due to handicaps. These events, especially with large fields as in the Stewards' Cup, the Royal Hunt Cup, the Cambridgeshire and the Cesarewitch, all open to older horses, may be book-ies' bonanzas and swell the Levy turnover, but they are basically poor races for poor horses and more so in the three-year-old category.

It followed that a good horse off, say, the nine stone mark in the Free Handicap and just below classic standard, would be unfairly burdened in handicaps and there were insufficient weight-for-age races of any value for such an animal to contest. The committee recommended, wisely enough, that while the classic races were supreme, the programme for three-year-olds should be supplemented by regular weight-for-age races of adequate value over distances from a mile to a mile and three-quarters.

The knotty problem of encouraging owners to keep horses in training at four and over was tackled, in the interest of counteracting the tendency to retire good horses to stud before they have been properly tested. Sadly, this has not proved to be of general advantage. Some top-class animals have remained in training as entires at four and five, but overall commercial considerations have held sway, a theme dating back to the Aga Khan in the thirties and for-ties and unlikely to change tune.

A filly is a different matter, but the leading colts can now be subjected to such a demanding season, starting with the classic trials in April, the Guineas races in May, the Derby trials in the same month, the King George, the St

Leger, the Arc, the Breeders' Cup and finally the Japan Cup and the Washington International. All are options over an eight month period of intensive competition, almost to the point that a four-year-old career may seem unthinkable.

This matter was regarded as critical by the Racing Reorganisation Committee of 1943, but it appears that no legislation or prize money criteria can find a solution.

Finally in equine terms, or as the committee's report puts it 'the horse itself', the committee recommended that sprinters should have a series of five and six furlong weight-for-age races spread over the whole season.

This was easily achieved and what might be described as the Heavy Brigade of racing, usually well endowed with the traditional bottom of a cook and the head of a lady, are well accommodated.

A comparison with the French pattern of racing concluded that, although they had achieved significant success in the period since the war, there was 'little evidence that they (the French) have succeeded in increasing the speed or general performance of the thoroughbred', but this apparent paradox presumably engaged the minds of the committee when they looked at the allocation of fixtures for the 'great races'.

They suggested that the ideal date for the Derby would be 8th or 10th June, acknowledging that Royal Ascot would have to be put back to 22nd or 23rd June; also that the 'French races' and the Irish Derby would be affected and the Newmarket Spring meeting would have to be later. Taking cognisance of the problems, the committee recommended some consideration to these proposals, 'if we are to do our best for the thoroughbred'. It is a matter of regret that these eminently sensible ideas were not implemented before the International Pattern became too set, although it is a little ironic that it took permission for Sunday racing to move the Derby to 9th June in what became the Saturday of Derby Weekend, as opposed to Derby Week (now put back again).

The report was far reaching, embracing a new scale of apprentice allowances, some caustic comments on plates and sellers and enthusing over mixed meetings of flat and National Hunt racing. This may have been a belated gesture to the National Hunt Committee as the report gives 'the winter game' a fairly short shrift. Although mixed meetings were popular at the time, and rightly so in the eyes of the racing buff, most of them have since been abandoned as Jackpot and Placepot punters found it difficult to grapple with combined jumping and flat form.

The committee encouraged local stewards to take a more vigilant approach and suggested that commercially sponsored races 'should not be taken into account of the Pattern of racing as they cannot be considered permanent'. Wise words, and although the recommendations of the Norfolk Committee not only formed the main elements of the existing Pattern and were influential both in revisions of the Rules of Racing and the allocation of prize money by the Levy Board, commercialism won the day with regard to sponsorship, principally because of a short-sighted financial policy by some racecourses which went unchecked by the Jockey Club.

As an outcome of the report, a Race Planning Committee was appointed under the chairmanship of Lord Porchester (now Lord Carnarvon) in May 1967. Subsequently, 131 races were adopted as 'Pattern races' but by 1976 the number had been reduced to one hundred. Today, the figure is 117.

This philosophy was endorsed by the Benson Committee, chaired by Sir Henry Benson (now Lord Benson) in June 1968, which concluded that 'Pattern races are those races which are necessary to provide a comprehensive system of tests for the best horses of various ages over various distances in accordance with the officially accepted Pattern of racing', going on to confirm that Pattern races set the standards for British racing and encourage the breeding of the highest grade of bloodstock, and 'the main prizes for flat racing should be awarded for the Pattern races'.

So far, so good. Liaison with the French avoided clashes of similar races and annual meetings of the International Pattern Committees of Ireland, Germany and Italy together with the founder countries, Great Britain and France, became the norm – North America holding a watching brief.

This liaison was continued when the Group system became inevitable after the French raised objections as to the comparatively low level of prize money in Britain in the 1960s. 'Grouping' enabled the winners of important British races to compete in similar events in France with small penalties or no penalties at all. The French were all for closing such races to foreign competitors except for those on strict weight-for-age terms, but the introduction of Group races saved the day.

Thus, in 1971, Pattern races were divided into Groups I, II and III according to their intrinsic importance as tests of racehorses rather than their monetary value, and penalties assessed on the basis of victories gained in the various Group events.

This arrangement, which still holds good today, defined Group I as 'championship races, including classic races, in which horses meet on weight-for-age terms with no penalties or allowances'. Group II was limited to races 'just below championship standard in which there may be some penalties and allowances', while Group III consists of races 'of mainly domestic interest, including classic trials, which are required to complete the series of tests for the best horses'.

The Joint Racing Board report on the Pattern of Racing published in 1975, concluded not unreasonably that the Group system was the saviour of international racing, but warned against the dangers of confusing the changes of race names and emphasised that the Pattern races should be protected from encroachment, in terms of prize money, by non-Pattern races including handicaps.

The question of sponsorship was also examined, and the view expressed that the aims of people or firms who contribute to prize money in return for advertising would not always be at one with the requirements of the Pattern. It was a point well taken but in the event commercial forces have had little effect on the structure of races, which is as it should be: as the report suggests, the pattern of racing and the logical series of tests proposed by the Norfolk Committee, accepted by both the Club and the Levy Board, while attracting international approval, would crumble in a few years if sponsors were allowed to manipulate the Pattern.

On the issue of the names of races, the Club were less fortunate. Despite agreement at the winter meeting of the Jockey Club in 1975 that in future no changes should be made to the names of any Pattern races except for the addition of a prefix or suffix, with mandatory referrals to the Jockey Club in the case of Group I or II events and to the Stewards in the case of Group III, such changes, 'more honour'd in the breach than the observance', have caused a good deal of confusion. This is notable at Goodwood, where the commercial tail might be said to wag the racing dog with an unacceptable frequency.

CHAPTER 14

A Tale of Two Charters and Back to Basics

The Norfolk Committee made no bones about the importance of Newmarket, home of the Jockey Club and the Headquarters of Racing since the mid-eighteenth century, stating, '... In our view, it has a special priority and must at all costs be maintained for the breeding, training and racing of horses. It may not, in the eyes of everyone, be considered a very accessible place, but should be given a priority for the maintenance of our industry against any claims that may be made for housing or any other form of industry.'

All very well and still true today, but by the early 1960s Newmarket was an obvious target for 'urban overspill', in the ghastly jargon of the time. Three thousand Londoners were eventually accepted by the West Suffolk County Council. The nettle of over-population which all rural areas had to grasp in a way unequalled since the wartime days of the urban evacuee children, gave Newmarket an extra sting; city dwellers were not used to living cheek by jowl with large animals, and land used for the breeding and training of the thoroughbred would have to be relinquished; the soft whinny of the foal give way to the raucous radio and the nasal whine of the noisy child.

The County Council's Planning Department and the Newmarket Urban District Council listed several studs close to the centre of the town which would then be taken over and built upon. The Jockey Club demurred pointing out that 'all the necessary development could take place in the Cheveley Park area, where seventy-five acres were available', but conceded that one of the studs nominated, Scaltback, had fallen into virtual disuse and that another, Brickfields, was probably going to be rendered useless by a planned by-pass road, and therefore were happy for the newcomers to be housed in one thousand new dwellings, within earshot of the comforting hum of traffic and the familiar squeal of the police sirens.

So far, all well and good, and the owner of Brickfields, Andrew Johnstone, was happy to agree to the sale. However, the Jockey Club owned the Hamilton Stud and they were anxious to raise cash for the Rowley and July courses,

rightly disdaining any largesse from the Levy Board which at that time was providing precious little anyway. Thus, Hamilton was to be developed.

If the mills of national government grind slowly and grind exceeding small, the mills of local administration are snails making face powder. By 1965 the County Council was speaking of 20,000 newcomers, as opposed to 17,000 in 1961, with a swelling to 28,000 by the millennium. The Council demanded four studs to be put to residential use.

On the Severals.

Understandably, this stuck in the craw of the Jockey Club, which wanted to protect Newmarket as a training centre. Much politicking followed with trainers, breeders, bloodstock agents and the sales company, Tattersall's, all brought into the fray. The Club did not wish for a public inquiry, and accordingly a 'Newmarket Charter' was drawn which represented at best an uneasy compromise.

Like most such, it failed, although bristling with good intentions: protecting the sport, expand-

*Top: Park Paddocks –
a sale.*

*Centre: Dutch Bank
Newmarket.*

Bottom: The Limekilns.

Rowley Mile Stand, Trainers Stand and Birdcage.

ing local employment and additional finance for local amenities. In the end, kickback killed the charter. A local and vocal group called the Newmarket Society consisting of farmers, breeders and trainers formed a curious alliance with local politicians headed by Kenneth Kemp-Turner, who is still active in Newmarket affairs, to defeat the purpose of the charter which was essentially an agreement to contain overspill on the lines of a deal negotiated with the Greater London Council in 1966. But there were fears that new businesses would attract employment away from racing with higher wages, and the rates, rents and jobs of the indigenous population should be protected.

Eventually Brickfield was developed and the Jockey Club sold Hamilton principally to provide the extensive range of stables which now line the Hamilton Road, thus relieving the pressure of the equine population on the town.

Jockeys mounting for the Cesarewitch Stakes.

The Club had done its best, and the resulting free-for-all has not changed the character of Newmarket to any great extent. Horse walks guide the animals and their riders as they thread their way from one side of the town to the other and they are safe on the minor streets as the author can testify since strings clatter past his door in the early a.m. with that entrancing clip-clop which in its way reflects the romance of racing.

Returning to the national scene, the Royal Charter effectively sprang from the Benson Committee report of 1968, which was concerned with racing as an industry rather than a sport. The Chairman was Sir Henry (later Lord) Benson, a distinguished chartered accountant with a strong record in public affairs who was later elected to the Jockey Club. His fellow members were Lord Abergavenny, a former Steward of the National Hunt Committee and to be Her majesty's Representative at Royal Ascot, Sir Rex Cohen and Major W D Gibson, a skilled Turf administrator and a fine amateur rider over fences, winning the Grand Military Gold Cup on four occasions.

The report was inevitably critical of the low level of finance in racing and in particular of the poor prize money compared to our principal rivals in France, who at that time were cheerfully plundering our few financially worthwhile races. Other problems highlighted were bad incomes for stable staff, declining racecourse attendances and low returns for breeders.

Benson was also concerned about the number of Turf boards and various vested interests all pulling in different directions.

Not for the first time, a new Racing Authority was mooted, with responsibility for raising and spending the Levy while its members represented most aspects of the racing industry – with trainers excepted as they were licensed by the Club. As with the British Horseracing Board today, this would to some extent reduce the responsibilities of the Jockey Club, especially as to finance. All income, including the Tote, would be the charge of the Authority.

The Jockey Club Committee Room.

It goes without saying that Lord Wigg opposed Benson, as he considered that the proposed Authority would simply be the Jockey Club 'writ large', although paradoxically he found much in the report to admire. Even so his unfounded suspicions were unhelpful and proved yet again how difficult it was, with the best will in the world, for the Jockey Club to reform itself from within during the eccentric political atmosphere of the sixties.

The Rothschild Commission on Gambling which reported in 1978 also came down in favour of a British Horseracing Authority, a proposition supported by the Club, and in general the report of the Commission paved a way for the Jockey Club to progress in the aftermath of the roaring inflation and economic stagnation which unhappily was the logical produce of the political incompetence and *lasse-faire* fudging by national government during one of the most decadent periods in English history.

The Dining Room.

Rothschild was too wide-reaching for its own good and few of the Commission's recommendations were implemented, but it gave the Jockey Club a chance to clear the air, which the stifling of the Benson report had prevented. As a result, a plethora of boards, committees and confederations had grown up, concerned and in some cases effective but not unified. However, in their favour it must be said that independent organisations such as the Bloodstock and Racehorse Industries Confederation (BRIC) were important and demonstrated the malaise of the industry.

All this was against the background of the Royal Charter which had been granted in 1970 and was the brainchild of Lord Porchester (now Lord Carnarvon). In the uncertain political atmosphere of the time, Porchester could see which way the wind was blowing as Chairman of the Sports Council's Planning Committee in 1965.

The National Playing Fields Association was in danger of being abolished by Denis Howell, then Minister of Sport. The Association was mostly funded by private contributions, and was a ripe target for socialist dogma. Porchester pointed out to Howell that as the NPFA had a Royal Charter, naturally enough since the Association was a favourite interest to HRH The Duke of Edinburgh, the NPFA could not be abolished.

It occurred to Lord Porchester that if the Jockey Club, following amalgamation with the National Hunt Committee, could obtain a Charter, this would protect forever the ruling body which had served the sport for over two centuries.

The advantage of the Charter was security and a bulwark against enforced change by ill-formed outsiders. The disadvantages were and remain that any modification, however trivial, requires Privy Council permission.

The Charter was a shrewd move; on the one hand, it could be altered, albeit laboriously, to accommodate a Racing Authority such as suggested by Benson, and at the same time it kept the enemy at bay. This administrative equivalent of boiling oil worked well for racing and ultimately allowed the sport to make its own decisions and be subject to none save HM The Queen and Parliament.

The 7th Earl of Carnarvon, as Lord Porchester is now, has served racing well since he was elected to the Jockey Club in 1964. He has been the Queen's

The paddock.

The Royal Stand in 1843.

racing manager since 1969, is a past-President of the Thoroughbred Breeders' Association and a former chairman of the Flat Race Pattern Committee. As a life-long friend of The Queen he was ideally placed for his advocacy of the Royal Charter; after all, Her Majesty is a patron of the Jockey Club. As an owner-breeder he has enjoyed success with such animals as Hiding Place, Smuggler, Matinée, Kittyhawk, Little Wolf and Lemon Soufflé.

Lord Carnarvon's distinguished service compares well with the other Jockey Club Titans of the post-war period. The two dominant figures were the 16th Duke of Norfolk and Major-General Sir Randle Feilden, both of whom have appeared in previous chapters. The Duke was an enthusiastic owner-breeder, both stable and stud being established near his home at Arundel Castle. It cannot be said that he achieved much success in the highest class, with the exception of Ragstone which he bred to win the Gold Cup at Ascot in 1974.

The grandstand and course.

It must have been a proud moment for the man who had modernised Ascot and made it second to none among European racecourses. Together with Sir John Crocker Bulteel, his outstanding Clerk of the Course, Norfolk founded the King George VI and the Queen Elizabeth Stakes. It was the first £100,000 event to be staged in Britain and second only to the Prix de l'Arc de Triomphe as the premiere race in the European calendar for three-year-olds and upwards.

The Duke served as Ascot Representative for the monarch from 1945 to 1972 and preserved the elegance of the Royal Meeting whilst not denying the trend of post-war social life. As an administrator, he brought to racing all the enthusiasm which he devoted to the affairs of his home county of Sussex and wartime service as Joint Parliamentary Secretary to the Minister of Agriculture. The Duke was a Steward and Vice-Chairman of the Turf Board and also the principal motivator of two of the most important inquiries into racing affairs in the post-war years; the Norfolk Committee on the Pattern of Racing in 1965 and the 1961 report on doping.

Racing was not Norfolk's only sporting interest and when he managed the MCC team which toured the antipodes in the winter of 1962-63 (a good winter not to be in England, one might add) it probably gave him as much pleasure as his countless successes on the racecourse.

Sir Randle 'Gerry' Feilden was an equally efficient administrator of the Turf, but in a manner more forceful and direct than Norfolk. He was not an instinctive racing enthusiast, no great horseman and had a stronger penchant for other field sports such as shooting, but his interest was kindled as a student at Cambridge, when he backed Charley's Mount to win at Newmarket at 100/1.

After a distinguished military career, Feilden retired in 1949, but had already become an owner in collaboration with the Duke of Norfolk, a close friend, and his horses were trained at Arundel. Sir Randle became a Steward in 1952 and served a second period between 1959 and 1961. He was Senior Steward in 1954 and 1961 and again in 1965. He was also Chairman of the Turf Board until he was succeeded as Senior Steward by Lord Leverhulme in 1973.

Feilden was a reformer in a blunt practical way which became increasingly effective and necessary during a most turbulent period in racing history, not always assisted by the behaviour of Lord Wigg. Sir Randle's downright approach appealed to the racing public, and his streamlining of the Jockey Club's administrative systems made the sport less mysterious and more acceptable to the increasingly sophisticated demands of the punter. He continued public duties after he left office and was Chairman of Cheltenham racecourse and also of the Stable Lads' Welfare Trust.

Lord Howard de Walden was Senior Steward in 1957, 1964 and between 1976 and 1979. Sometimes described as the 'Bertie Wooster' of racing, nothing could be further from the truth although he has an ability to see the lighter side – which would be an advantage in some other administrators. His 1964 Committee report defined for the first time the modern distinction between the sport and its regulation and racing as an industry, anticipating a likely clash with an unsympathetic Levy Board chairman.

Other far-reaching propositions were the amalgamation with the National Hunt Committee to give racing a warmth of unity in an increasingly chilly world, which was an essential requirement of the Royal Charter, and the suggestion of an advisory council which led to the Horseracing Advisory Council, in turn the Industry Committee with three seats on the British Horseracing Board.

A prominent owner-breeder who names his horses with superb imagination, thus indicating a mind perhaps not that far from the Wodehouse idiom in the literary sense, Lord Howard achieved a lifetime ambition when Slip Anchor won the Derby in 1985. One of de Walden's best named horses was Gondolier, by Slip Anchor out of Grimpola; ten minutes on the Grande Canale will testify to the neatness of that appellation.

Another with a well-developed funny bone is Colonel Sir Piers Bengough for many years Her Majesty's Representative at Royal Ascot and a Steward for four years before serving as a Jockey Club nominee on the Levy Board for a similar term, during the Chairmanships of Sir Desmond Plummer and Sir Ian Trethowan.

He was originally elected as a member of the National Hunt Committee in 1965, as became one of the finest soldier-riders of his time. Bengough won the Grand Military Gold Cup at Sandown on four occasions, on Joan's Rival in 1960 and then enjoyed three successes with Charles Dickens in 1970, 71 and 72. It was therefore appropriate that, as a licensing Steward, he granted the first licences for women to ride over fences under Rules.

Not all Jockey Club grandees were happy with the amalgamation of the Club and the steeplechasing authority in 1968. Lord Sefton, finding that his race glasses had 'gone missing' at Newmarket, fumed: 'What can one expect now we're in with the National Hunt Committee?' But as Sir Piers points out, the National Hunt Stewards brought practical experience to racing in terms of riding and training, crafts in which the flat race stewards were not always so well versed.

Bengough was delighted to find, when he was appointed a Steward of the Jockey Club, that four of them, Lord Leverhulme, then Senior Steward, Lord Manton, Captain Miles Gosling and himself had all been at one time or another under the care of A K Kerry, their housemaster at Eton.

Sir Piers was a major influence in the founding of the British Racing School for apprentices and was Chairman of the Disciplinary Committee when such matters as abuse of the whip, the reformation of Rule 153 on disqualification for improper race riding, and doping were in the forefront of the racing world. Doping in particular achieved notoriety as a result of the Aliysa case when the Club had to defend themselves against the mighty wealth of the

Aga Khan and his batteries of lawyers. In the end, justice was done and seen to be done. Today, Sir Piers is a member of the Disciplinary Review Committee.

John Hislop certainly had a considerable experience of race-riding and training. He was elected a member of the Club in 1971 following the record breaking exploits of his home-bred colt, Brigadier Gerard, and was an excellent steward both locally and nationally. A modest man, he was champion amateur rider on the flat in 1938 and 1939, prior to military service in the Sussex Yeomanry and with 'Phantom', being awarded the MC for his bravery.

Perhaps Hislop had to display even greater courage to finish third to Caughoo on Kami in the 1947 Grand National, in the days when it was a feat of horsemanship to get round, let alone be placed. He was again champion amateur on the flat from 1946 to 1956.

As a breeder, he was adamant in his defence of British stock. He refused huge sums from abroad to keep his beloved Brigadier at home, and was equally firm in declaring that the European Breeders' Fund, a scheme to provide breeders' prizes for the owners of dams of winners, funded in principle by a premium equal to the cost of a nomination to the sire deposited by the stallion owner, was 'illogical, unethical and dangerous in principle'.

Hislop's view was that the scheme involved a degree of blackmail, and he resented that the matter had never been discussed at a Jockey Club meeting. John was equally scornful of the notion of co-registration with the American Breeders' Cup fund, which admitted European animals to the richly endowed US races and permitted American produce to race in EBF events on this side of the 'herring pond'. He described the Breeders' Cup as the 'Bleeders' Cup', as unsound horses were racing on medication.

Hislop resigned from the TBA but remained a member of the Jockey Club. Apart from his skill in the saddle, and his achievements as a breeder and administrator, his most lasting contribution lies in his literary work.

Author of the Jockey Club pamphlet on the correct use of the whip, which was the only official guideline against abuse before the matter became one of public concern in the eighties, John Hislop edited *The British Racehorse* for many years and

Hislop, nearest camera, taking the last to go on to win at Windsor. He was an even more outstanding jockey on the flat and was leading amateur from 1946-55.

was racing correspondent for both The *Observer* and the *News of the World*. His self-deprecating autobiographies, *Far From a Gentleman*, *Anything But a Soldier* and *Hardly a Jockey* are classics of Turf literature. As this author has good cause to remember, he always found time to dispense help and advice to junior journalists.

In the high days of Feilden, Norfolk, de Walden, Hislop and Bengough, there were no Jockey Club Standing Committees; if something needed to be done, justice meted out or decisions made, jockeys, trainers and others were called in (and in some cases called to account) as and when required by the exigencies of the sport. All this was to change as racing strove to keep pace with the 'street-wise' philosophies of the eighties.

It was a question of attempting to bond the various associations, some of which had been going for many years, such as the Racehorse Owners Association and the TBA. Accordingly, the Horseracing Advisory Council was formed in 1980. As the name implies, HAC, as it soon came to be known in the jargon of the press, had influence but no executive authority. It was itself spawned by the Racing and Breeding Liaison Committee, combining the interests of racecourses, breeders and owners.

HAC took over the responsibilities of the Bloodstock and Racehorse Industries Confederation, founded in 1975 and the concept of John Winter, a leading trainer in Newmarket, and John Corbett, a well-known bloodstock agent. The brief of BRIC was to deal with the slump in the bloodstock industry, and in particular VAT on bloodstock. In this sense it was well ahead of its time and was a strong influence both internally and externally in the politics of racing during the seventies when it must be remembered that inflation was running at 24 per cent under the benign administration of Harold (pound in your pocket or your purse) Wilson.

The Club appreciated BRIC's efforts, but chose to form their own body with similar aims, the Racing Industries Liaison Committee, which ran alongside the Joint Associations Liaison Committee dating back to 1964.

It was all too much. Following an extraordinary and complex conference staged by the Levy Board at Sandown in 1975, HAC provided a rationalisation for all the many vested interests in racing. HAC was originally constituted with a non-executive General Council including multifarious representatives, and a simple Executive Committee.

It was a useful forum, enjoying the support of the All-Party Parliamentary Committee on Racing, the Home Secretary and, of course, the Jockey Club. Much of the credit for both the organisation and its effectiveness must be given to Stanley Jackson, the first Secretary and the second Chairman, Major-General Bernard Penfold. General Penfold was brought in after the swift arrival and departure of Phil Bull, who was originally appointed to the Chair.

CHAPTER 15

The Valentino years
Women, the Whip and the
Sheikhs of Araby

For several generations, women had no official or formal part in racing, outside of members of the Royal Family. They could not train, ride in races or even own horses; female owners such as the Duchess of Montrose and Lady de Bathe, better known as Lily Langtry, had to race under 'noms de course' as 'Mr Manton' or 'Mr Jersey'.

The Sex Discrimination Act of 1975 was to change such nonsense for ever, although women as owners had been admitted long before. Gainsborough in 1918 became the first Derby winner credited to a woman when he won for Lady James Douglas, and in 1937 both the winner and second were owned by females. Midday Sun was owned by Mrs Betty Miller, and the runner-up, Sandsprite, ran in the colours of Mrs Florence Nagle – and thereby hangs a tail.

Mrs Nagle both owned and trained Sandsprite, but the licence had to be held by a private trainer, Hugh Powney. After the war, Florence Nagle set up a racing stable at Westerlands near Petworth in Sussex, where she also had a stud. The property was formerly owned by Lord Woolavington, and both the training and breeding enterprises prospered, with many of Mrs Nagle's winners such as Westerlands Champagne, Westerland Chalice, Westerlands Rosebud, Gelert and West Partisan, descending from Westerlands Rose, a prolific broodmare by Columbo out of Rose of England. Columbo had won the 2,000 Guineas for Lord Glanely in 1934 and Rose of England took the Oaks for the same owner in 1930.

Mrs Nagle also trained Elf-Arrow to win the Liverpool St Leger in 1959 and seven other races for her friend Miss F Newton-Deakin, but the ludicrous prohibition on the licensing of women trainers produced pure garbage in the otherwise excellent publication *Horses in Training.* Under 'Mrs F Nagle, Petworth' appeared in brackets 'Licence may be held by W H Stickley'. May be? Miss Nora Wilmot, in the same unfortunate position, had to rely on a licence held by R H Swash for her training establishment in Berkshire. Both Stickley and Swash were head lads and Mrs Louie Dingwall trained her first winner in the head lad's name in 1932.

These ladies, and eventually everyone else, wearied of this silly pretence and Mrs Nagle brought a case against the Jockey Club. Finally, she emerged victorious and following a verdict in the Court of Appeal in July 1966, the Club were forced to grant training licences to women. The presiding judge, Lord Justice Denning, observed, 'If she is to carry on her trade without stooping to subterfuge she has to have a training licence.'

The subsequent achievements of women such as Jenny Pitman, Lady Herries, Mary Reveley, Lynda Ramsden and Sally Hall, to name only a few, proved conclusively enough that on the training front women were and are equal to the best. Riding was perhaps another matter; although women had ridden successfully in point-to-points for many years, racing between the flags was, rightly, an extension of the hunting field and lacked the hard competition of professional racing. Some good judges thought that race-riding, and National Hunt racing in particular, was too dangerous for the fair sex.

The first two women to win steeplechases under National Hunt rules – Diana and Jane Thorne in 1978. Jane was later a close second on Spartan Missile in the Whitbread Gold Cup.

As always, David Nicholson was the most forthright, being especially critical of the eventing style amongst women riders, which he described as, 'The fanny crouch: legs back, bottoms up, all bust and backside.' As Nicholson later coached HRH The Princess Royal for her successful career as a race-rider, one wonders if these sentiments were made clear to the Princess, while Lester Piggott, who should know as he possesses one of the best known posteriors in

Dressed up only? A gimmick to promote the Irish Sweeps Derby.

racing, considered that the female bottom was 'the wrong shape' for jockey-ship.

But progress came, albeit a stage at a time. The first modern race for women riders, the Goya Stakes, was run on the flat at Kempton Park on 6th May 1972 and won by Meriel Tufnell on her mother's Scorched Earth at 50/1. Racing over obstacles was still taboo, and remained so until the Sex Discrimination Act three years later, but races confined to female amateur jockeys became a regular feature of flat racing cards.

Sponsors were particularly keen, perhaps because the novelty of attractive girls in flimsy riding kit, wearing boots and carrying whips, had a slightly 'Naughty nineties' smack about it and certainly distracted the punters on, say, a dull day at Doncaster, most of whom disagreed with L. Piggott's anatomical theories.

Halfway through the 1975-76 National Hunt season, the Discrimination Act came into force. On 30th January 1976, Muriel Naughton became the first woman to take part in a steeplechase, the Spittall Hill Amateur Riders' Handicap at Ayr. Three weeks later, Sue Horton, better known in the point-to-point field by her maiden name of Alston, rode Le Toy in an amateur riders' handicap hurdle at Ascot, but it was Diane Thorne (now Henderson) who provided the first happy ending when steering Ben Ruler home to win the Nimrod Hunters' Chase at Stratford on Avon.

The Act gave the Jockey Club a few headaches. Strictly speaking, the Club did not have to grant licences to women riders to enable them to compete with men as Clause 44 of the Act provided that sporting contests could be confined to one sex if 'the physical strength, stamina or physique of the average woman puts her at a disadvantage with the average man'.

Taking the view that the horse did 80 per cent of the work during a race, and that therefore race-riding was not a straight man-against-woman contest (as would be the case in a boxing match, for instance, or a tennis tournament) the Club proceeded.

The Dowager Duchess of Montrose — otherwise known as Six Mile Bottom. Rumoured to have had a passion for Fred Archer she was a much loved representative of the fairer sex on the racecourses of England though the trainer Alex Taylor was the only man allowed into her bedroom. On one occasion she stormed out of a church when the vicar prayed for fine weather for the harvest not realising that the Duchess's St. Leger runner was a mud lark.

Lady Halifax, member of the Jockey Club.

An unexpected swerve came when it was realised that the Act, naturally enough, covered all forms of discrimination. No longer could the Club cosily provide 'ladies only' races which gave stable girls an equal chance, since although they were paid employees they were granted amateur permits for ladies' races, the idea of mixed races not being entertained prior to the Act. This policy encouraged girls to work in stables and a weight allowance encouraged trainers to give them rides. However, the Act, like all such, including the Race Relations legislation, was inevitably and equally sauce for the goose and sauce for the gander, in some ways striking against the very people it was intended to help.

In future, the women would have to compete on equal terms against men. Stable girls would be regarded in the same light as stable lads, ie professionals. The flat racing girls had suffered a severe blow, but with the help of the Lady Jockey's Association and the Equal Opportunities Commission, a temporary way forward was found.

Dennis Howell, then Minister for Sport, a role in which he experienced rather more success than in his later comic opera appointment as 'Minister for Rain' following the drought of 1976, met with Lord Leverhulme, the then Jockey Club Secretary, Charles Weatherby, and Diana Bissill and Vivien Kaye from the LJA.

It was agreed to change the Rules in order that a paid employee could work with horses, and so long as a professional jockey's licence had never been granted, revert to amateur status one year after relinquishing such employment. Also, the Club allowed stable girls to ride in races confined to Lady Jockeys' Association members until 1978. Since the concept of 'Club' races was already observed in such events as Military Meetings and by the International Association for male riders, FEGENTRI, it was further agreed that the LJA, as a recognised club, could stage events confined to the female sex, although flat races previously confined to men of amateur status had to become open to either sex with the exception of Club races.

This gave women a foothold in the world of race-riding, but since 1978 they have had to plough their own furrow against the men on a professional basis. The way has not been easy; some like Lorna Vincent and Alex Greaves have achieved fame and distinction, but although all-weather racing has provided an unanticipated opportunity for girl jockeys on the dull and featureless sand tracks, the higher stakes continue to be denied to them. Overall, it seems that owners and trainers prefer male jockeys and that includes women trainers and owners.

Meanwhile, the Jockey Club accepted its first female members and Mrs Priscilla Hastings (elected in 1977), Mrs Susan Abbott (1989), Miss Mary Gordon-Watson (1991), Miss Judy Thompson (1984), Miss Kirsten Rausing

(1992), Mrs Brudenell-Bruce, Mrs Embiricos and Mrs Johnson-Houghton and others represent the distaff side of the Club today.

Unhappily, the ugly and unattractive side of racing also emerged in the mid to late seventies. This was excessive and improper use of the whip, an emotional issue which had lain more or less dormant for decades, but was certainly nothing new, as this anonymous contribution to the sporting press in 1885 testifies:

> Two or three well applied strokes of the whip in the last hundred yards or so means probably the gaining of a length. As long as the horse can keep his place or avoid losing it without the whip, that dangerous implement should not be raised.

This was strong stuff, bearing in mind the attitude to animals and their welfare just over 100 years ago, when many horses pulling carts and drays were not always considerately treated.

Admiral Rous's views expressed in 1866 in his book *The Laws and Practice of Horse Racing* have been recorded in Chapter Five and the burden of his comments suggested that improper use of the whip impaired the horse's winning chance, but not all Victorian jockeys subscribed to that theory. Fred Archer, one of the greatest jockeys ever to sit in a weighing chair, was notoriously heavy-handed with the whip, to the extent that he was badly savaged by a vengeful animal on Newmarket Heath following a double dose of the 'Archer Treatment'.

On the other hand, George Fordham, who won sixteen classic races and was champion jockey fourteen times, was very sparing and rarely used his whip at all, and never on a two-year-old.

Between the wars, riding standards were extremely high and only occasionally was a rider summoned by the stewards if the punishment received by his mount was clearly too severe or if the horse was badly marked.

This happy and civilised way of behaviour continued into the post-war years, but as the senior riders retired they were replaced by a more aggressive breed of jockey, representing the softer social ambience of the period who had never experienced the benefits of a harsh and tough apprenticeship, and adopted a literally more cavalier attitude to the sport.

The Jockey Club have often been accused of pandering to the townie television viewer who has no equestrian experience whatever and who reacts in an over-emotional way to the sight of horses being whipped in races, and that the Instructions (H9) on the use of the whip with their attendant penalties are largely a cosmetic exercise to pacify the ignorant.

To some extent this may be true as television is a great magnifier, and no sporting administration would wish for its public relations to be damaged by the blatant thuggery of a few. Equally there can be no doubt that riding standards in respect of misuse of the whip reached a nadir in the seventies, as the

Good use of the whip in a close finish.

author can vouch from his experiences as a commentator for the former *World of Sport* programme.

On Saturday afternoons *World of Sport* presented the ITV Seven – as its name implies seven races from two courses making up a multiple bet. It was unashamed bookie fodder, and as only one or two races from either course represented anything resembling good quality racing, the remaining four or five events were invariably dross, with bad horses often ridden by bad jockeys competing for worse prizes.

One frequently had to observe the miserable sight of a wretched animal being belaboured by a rider whose style was better suited to a cattle round-up on the plains of Montana, long after any chance of success had gone. This was particularly evident in poor National Hunt races, and public reaction was understandable and inevitable.

Matters came to a head at the televised (BBC) Festival meeting at Cheltenham in March 1980, when two Irish jockeys, Tommy Ryan and Joe Byrne, gave a notorious display of whip abuse and subsequently received long suspensions. It was now evident that the comments made for some years by experienced racegoers were correct; misuse of the whip had gone too far.

As a result of the events at Cheltenham, the Jockey Club issued a statement defining 'Improper Riding', eg hitting a beaten horse, using the whip after passing the post or hitting horses with 'unreasonable frequency'.

The very fact that the Club had to make such a statement of the obvious illustrated the depth of the problem. Four years later, in 1984, regulations were introduced limiting the length and diameter of the whip, but they were to little avail. The ensuing four years saw an increase in the vigorous behaviour of riders when 'encouraging' their mounts and by March 1988 it had become necessary to toughen up the restrictions covering unnecessary use, misuse and excessive use whilst prescribing correct use. A ten stroke maximum, which would trigger a mandatory enquiry by the stewards was set and suspensions replaced fines as the recommended punishment for offenders.

Needless to say, the knights of the pigskin were up in arms and a half-day strike proved as futile as most and merely highlighted the case against them.

More action became necessary in November 1988, when it became obvious that some flat-race jockeys were hitting horses down the shoulder with the whip in the forehand position, presumably to avoid attracting attention with the backhand stroke. The shoulder stroke was prohibited except for very exceptional circumstances, mostly geared to safety. In 1989, racecourse veterinary surgeons were instructed to report incidents where blood had been drawn or there were excessive weals.

Brutalisation of their mounts by jockeys hopefully contained, in 1991 the Club commissioned a video demonstrating the correct use of the whip, but still the riders either did not get the message, or ignored it, and in September 1992 a meeting of the Disciplinary Committee decided to re-appraise the Whip Instruction, H9, and set up a working group under the chairmanship of Colonel Sir Piers Bengough. Jockeys, trainers, vets and Stewards' Secretaries were represented and those who gave evidence included the representatives of twelve overseas Turf authorities. This was invaluable, as the problem was now world-wide and Australia, New Zealand, South Africa, Germany, Ireland and some states in North America were having to address the subject.

The working party redefined some aspects of the Instruction; in particular the raising of the whip above shoulder height became illegal and further emphasis was placed on the training of apprentice jockeys and conditional riders, but the recommendation which caused most reaction was on the matter of the 'trigger' mechanism which prompted stewards of meetings to look at jockeys' riding.

The party suggested that the trigger should be reduced from ten strokes to eight or more, but the Disciplinary Committee decided on a more draconian approach, and reduced the level to six or more throughout the duration of a flat race or after the penultimate obstacle in a N.H. event.

Journalists who had never been within whacking distance of a cane, outlawed in most educational establishments for the last thirty years at least, delighted in the phrase 'six of the best' but in the event it worked in conjunction with a scale of stiffer penalties. At the end of the 1994 Turf season, the Jockey Club were able to announce that whip offences were down by a third.

The new regulations were introduced in July 1993. For the first six months there were 84 jockeys in breech of the instructions, a rate of 14 per month. During the ensuing extended ten month period from 1st January, the figure was 107 overall, or around ten offences monthly. Complaints from the public dropped away, and jockeys were no longer having to count; as one senior rider who had 641 rides in the season said, 'Now it all seems more natural – it's all part of the rhythm and the way you ride.'

Yes, indeed, and that is how it should always have been. Supporters of racing, one hopes, are glad that the modern Jockey Club have never lost sight of the fact that the most important contributor to the Turf is the horse.

So 'All's Well that Ends Well', but to confuse the metaphor, 'the condition on which God hath given liberty to man is eternal vigilance'. Never again should racing tolerate the brand of thuggery which has gone unchecked in several other sports, and in tackling the problem effectively after giving the jockeys every chance to reform themselves, the Jockey Club has again demonstrated its superiority in sporting administration.

The quest goes on, with continuing research into the specifications and design of the whip, which could provide an instrument of control without inflicting needless pain and injury. As for those riders who resisted humane measures for so long, perhaps Sir Nöel Coward was right when he asserted that their brains were too close to their bottoms.

A glance at the Directory of Stewards and Members of the Jockey Club will reveal the names of HH Prince Khalid bin Abdullah, HH Sheikh Mohammed bin Rashid, Mr Fahd Salman, H H Sheikh Hamdan bin Rashid al Maktoum, and H H Sheikh Maktoum bin Rashid al Maktoum; all are listed as Honorary Members. The senior is Prince Khalid, nominated in 1983 and the latest Fahd Salman in 1992, following the success of his colt Generous in the 1991 Derby.

Their presence reflects the huge impact made by Middle Eastern owners since 1976, when a filly called Hatta, a 6,200 guineas Newmarket Sales purchase, won the Molecomb Stakes at Goodwood for Sheikh Mohammed. Since then, they have won twenty-eight classic races in England and countless other top-class events.

Oil was not discovered in the Middle East until the early 20th century when it was exploited by the western powers to serve the increasingly mecha-

The wonderful rise of the Godolphin operation. Sheikh Mohammed with his trainer Hilal Ibrahim alongside Balanchine and Frankie Dettori.

nised world which emerged from the first world war. The desert installations were guarded by a military presence sustained by aerial patrols, and little oil wealth filtered down to the indigenous population.

However, in the post-Suez period of the late fifties, when the Canal was closed and Ferdinand de Lesseps and Benjamin Disraeli were turning in their graves while supertankers roamed the high seas, the Arabs ruthlessly exploited the discovery of 'black gold' in Abu Dhabi, in the Trucial States, now known as the United Arab Emirates and in Saudi Arabia.

The Organisation of Petroleum Exporting Countries, or OPEC, lost no time in taking advantage of an American administration already wracked by the war in Vietnam and a Britain weakened by years of inept government.

157

The mid-seventies inflation rate of 20 per cent plus was well fuelled by OPEC as they constantly increased the price of oil. By 1976, with an income of two billion dollars a year secure and rising for the OPEC nations, the Arabs were ready to enter British racing, later expanding to race in all leading European countries and the USA.

Given their enormous purchasing power the Arabs could hardly go wrong, although they had their failures; the $12,000,000 purchase, Snaafi Dancer was so slow he could hardly get out of his box, never saw a racecourse and proved useless at stud.

When the ill winds of recession were scattering the falling leaves of prosperity like used confetti along Newmarket High Street, the soothsayers feared for a withdrawal by the Arabs, faced with high VAT on their British purchases and training bills, while it seemed likely that Sheikh Mohammed would become a supplier of bloodstock rather than a buyer.

Eventually a VAT concession was negotiated, and in any event it is interesting to speculate on where they would have gone. In 1993, Italy was on the verge of bankruptcy led by corruption, French racing was facing a massive financial crisis, Germany was struggling with the huge cost of reunification and the USA waiting for the new-boy President to show his lengthy talents to the nation.

Fortunately, the Arabs stayed, and racing is the better for it. They are undemonstrative sportsmen, but true sportsmen nonetheless and they race fairly, openly and with dignity. Nothing could have proven the latter point more graphically than when Prince Kahlid Abdullah was confronted after the victory of Zafonic in the 1993 2,000 Guineas by a television reporter kneeling in mock obeisance; a gesture of appalling taste and designed for self-advertisement. Like Josef Stalin in a very different context, Prince Khalid merely smiled.

CHAPTER 16

Revolution!

by Michael Tanner

W e're in charge!' So declared the *Racing Post*'s banner headline of
Friday, 11 June 1993 above a photograph of the British
Horseracing Board: 'New era begins as BHB takes over.' After 241
years of single-handedly controlling British racing, the self-electing, self-per-
petuating oligarchy that was the Jockey Club had voluntarily relinquished
much of its power to a new body drawn from all corners of the racing industry which would be, in the words of the Senior Steward, Lord Hartington,
'Ultimately responsible' for directing the sport. Whilst the Jockey Club
retained day-to-day control of racing's discipline, conduct of a day's racing,
licensing, security and matters of overall integrity, responsibility for all major
policy decisions, encompassing fixtures and finance for example, passed to the
BHB. No wonder the *Racing Post's* reaction to the announcement of this blueprint for the future back in December 1991 had been the single word
'Revolution!'

In truth, the 'Revolution' had been coming for some time. In 1978, when
the Club's respected historian Roger Mortimer was describing its position as
'perhaps less assured than at any time in its history', the Royal Commission
on Gambling (echoing Benson's findings of 1968) had recommended the
establishment of a new British Horseracing Authority to assume most of the
Levy Board's functions and some of the Jockey Club's. The recommendation
fell on stony ground; ground already littered with the detritus of organisations
founded with the similarly grandiose intentions of easing and improving the
administration of British racing: BRIC (Bloodstock and Racehorse Industries
Confederation), JALC (Joint Association Liaison Committee); RILC (Racing
Industry Liaison Council). The outcome on this occasion was the Horserace
Advisory Council, very much a compromise.

Representatives for the general council and executive committee of the
HAC were duly elected in December 1979: the former included delegates
from all interested parties – with one exception. Conspicuously absent was
any representative of the bookmaking fraternity, whose participation merely

took the form of 'observer' status. Lord Wigg, for one, was unimpressed: 'The Jockey Club set up JALC, which was a phoney, and the RILC, which was no better. HAC is a sound idea which, like time and time again, the Jockey Club have stepped in and used for their own devices.'

The chairman of HAC would have the right to attend meetings of the Jockey Club Stewards and would subsequently take up one of the Jockey Club's three seats on the Levy Board, two roles which constituted a marked improvement on anything offered by RILC and other earlier incarnations. That first chairman was Phil Bull, the erudite – and forthright – founding father of the Timeform organisation. 'The function of the general council of the HAC,' he stated, 'is to provide a forum for the expression of the views of all the various sectional racing interests. The function of the executive committee is to have regard to the views of the various sectional interests voiced in general council meetings and to distil these views and co-ordinate them into policies to be pursued with the Levy Board the Jockey Club and Government. Government won't listen to us if we are divided and present our views independently.'

The Senior Steward's reaction to the possibility of HAC input eroding a measure of the Jockey Club's authority and power did little to nip Lord Wigg's argument in the bud. 'It is too early to judge whether the HAC will have a powerful influence on decision-making,' said John Macdonald-Buchanan. 'It should be remembered that the Jockey Club has executive power and all the responsibilities that go with it. The HAC, on the other hand, is an advisory body, not obliged to make decisions and not, therefore, carrying the responsibilities of decision-making. One of the problems is that the HAC is made up of entirely interested parties. So decision-making is somewhat difficult. I am very hopeful that HAC will become a really powerful influence in racing. I became Senior Steward when the idea was being recommended and I have done, although I say it myself, as much as anyone to get HAC off the ground. I think that they will be not only a powerful influence but also an extremely helpful influence to both the Jockey Club and the Levy Board – at least that's what I hope.'

The Senior Steward's hopes seemed to be dashed almost immediately. 'While the HAC has no executive powers in the racing set-up, it is by no means powerless,' wrote Bull in March 1980. 'It has at its disposal the most potent of all weapons, the power of the written and spoken word, three months later Bull resigned. That someone of his knowledge and authority appeared to have come so quickly to the conclusion that the HAC was unlikely to become an effective force severely undermined confidence in the new organisation's credibility. The *Sporting Life's* outspoken columnist Jack Logan (Sir David Llewellyn) labelled the HAC as nothing more than 'a costly and decorative facade behind which the Jockey Club can do exactly what they want... it is designed to give an impression of power-sharing.' Lord Wigg joined in: 'The papers they put forward are amateurish drivel... it has become

THE JOCKEY CLUB
AT WORK TODAY

*Stewards left to right:
Anthony Mildmay-White
(Disciplinary), Christopher
Sporborg (Finance), Sir
Thomas Pilkington (Senior
Steward) and Michael
Wates (Deputy Senior
Steward).*

wholly cosmetic, an instrument of the Jockey Club.'

After Bull's brief and tempestuous reign as chairman of the HAC, the tenures of Major-General Bernard Penfold and Sir Nevil Macready were relatively low-key. Throughout the 1980s the suspicion lingered that HAC's members, far from using the HAC as their intermediary, were still more inclined to lobby the Jockey Club via their own individual organisations. An additional slur concerned HAC's perceived inability to get the Jockey Club to alter course on any issue on which it had set its mind. 'With the advent of the HAC we started to consult ourselves to a standstill,' says David Pipe, who was the Jockey Club's manager of public relations from 1987 to October 1997. 'Everything took a long time because consultation was governed by the dates of the relative Stewards' and council meetings and was not just a matter of the two secretariats working together. However, there was a strong measure of agreement between the stewards and chairman of the HAC but often he was obliged to channel ideas which not only the Jockey Club but also some of his own members disagreed with. There was a lot of dissension within the HAC,

*Left to right: Michael
Henriques (Licensing),
David Oldrey and Robert
Waley-Cohen (Racecourse).*

but it was only on very rare occasions that the Jockey Club went against the HAC view, such as the question of Rule 153 covering interference, and those were the cases which were most publicly aired.' Five years into the HAC's existence *Pacemaker* magazine's publisher Nick Robinson concluded: 'Consultation has been increased yet there has been no erosion of the Club's power base. If the Jockey Club is to be justified in retaining its power, we must expect more positive leadership and a sign that not only is there a way to increase racing's prosperity but, perhaps more importantly, that there is a real will to do so.'

Was the HAC as toothless as Wigg, Logan and Robinson averred? Was it nothing more than a talking-shop and/or a Jockey Club puppy? 'We're not ballyhoo merchants,' explained Stanley Jackson, HAC's chief executive and secretary. 'Our principal role is to knock the rough edges off arguments, to stop abrasiveness between organisations and to eliminate confrontation. The net result is that if we're successful there's a lack of news. Really, we're the dullest association in racing. We're a healing organisation. Our job is to build bridges and keep open the lines of communication.' Perhaps there was too much talking, too much consultation and not enough action, but, whatever its deficiencies, HAC can at least lay claim to having helped build the biggest 'Bridge' of all, that spanning the Jockey Club and the British Horseracing Board.

Nick Robinson, for one, continued to berate the Jockey Club for its torpor: 'Lord Fairhaven's succession as Senior Steward appears to have continued the rather laid-back policy initiated by his predecessor, placing the Club more and more in the role of umpire over racing's various factions… despite brave words the Jockey Club has not moved forward fast enough under Lord Fairhaven's regime.' The Senior Steward was given space in Robinson's publication to mount a defence: 'Things in the racing world take an awful time. The decision-making process is very thorough, which is good. We may be accused of moving slowly but that is necessary because there are so many organisations involved, all of them important and each of them needing to have its say. Few things are as straightforward as they appear.'

Robinson was not the only publisher with a ready vehicle for voicing criticism. James Underwood, publisher and editor of *British and Irish Breeding Update,* was a loose cannon who could be, and frequently was, particularly caustic: 'I am an abolitionist simply because I think the Jockey Club is incorrigible. It is an atrophy of old forms of society which functioned when we had people at the top who did lead the country… but I think they are an anachronism in the sense that they are not people of any significance or importance yet they are trying to run the industry. They are merely acting as policemen. We want something more than policemen, we need a city council. We need some deliberations and debate. We need more professional business acumen put into running the sport.' Even Underwood, however, was not so blunt as certain members of the bookmaking world. Peter George of Ladbroke's reckoned: 'The problem with the Jockey Club is that they are stupid… and unsophisticated. They behave like a cottage industry.' Don Bruce of BOLA argued: 'We have always been prepared to co-operate. The trouble is that what the Jockey Club means by co-operation is "Pay us more".'

By the end of Lord Fairhaven's term as Senior Steward in 1989 racing's finances were as much a thorny issue as ever, a point he stressed in his valedictory address at the annual Gimcrack Dinner: 'There is a real danger that without a proper return from the betting industry's leviable turnover it will be difficult to sustain our present position, let alone invest in the future.' He concluded by saying: 'The diversity and complexity of future plans and programmes will pose a challenging test of leadership. The Jockey Club is well aware of what will be required.' The new Senior Steward would need a cool head and a steady hand if the Jockey Club was to steer racing toward the 21st century. The tiller was passed to 44-year-old Peregrine Andrew Morny Cavendish, the Marquis of Hartington.

Lord Fairhaven at his home, Anglesey Abbey.

Lord Hartington's record at the Jockey Club embraced two years as Steward and a seat on the Levy Board plus membership of the Race Planning Committee; he was also a trustee of the Ascot Authority, a member of the York Race Committee and had served as a steward at Ascot, York and Newbury; he had horses in training and owned the Side Hill Stud in Newmarket. Nevertheless, beyond the loftier reaches of the Turf, Hartington was comparatively unknown, causing Jack Logan to observe: 'Given the system of selection by the magic circle we have, his is an interesting and welcome choice. I have, however, only one nagging doubt. Life has taught me that it is no kindness to promote anyone too soon. He has, in fact, kept such a low profile that he will have been the subject to this report by a Colonel as a young subaltern: "The men will follow this officer anywhere if only out of curiosity." Logan was all for giving Hartington a chance to prove himself; his editor at the *Sporting Life,* Monty Court, gave no such licence: 'I can only

Cheltenham Races, Stewards of the Jockey Club. Left to right: Brigadier Andrew Parker Bowles, The Earl Cadogan, Marquess of Hartington, Major Michael Wyatt, Colonel Sir Piers Bengough, Sir John Barlow.

think that with him at the helm the Jockey Club looks set for a period of non-achievement tantamount to stagnation.' .

Lord Hartington's five years as Senior Steward (1989–1994) were marked by anything but "stagnation". He was a revelation. 'He is a great communicator,' says David Pipe. 'Straight away he wanted to meet the press and I arranged a day at his stud. It was the first time I'd really seen him in action with the press and I was most impressed. I can remember saying to myself: "I've got a winner here". He was clearly someone who could communicate with both Stewards and the media.' Hartington lost no time in refitting the ship. Even before taking office he presided over a specially formed committee set up by his predecessor, Lord Fairhaven, to examine not only the Club's future role in the administration and financing of racing but also how its message could be more effectively conveyed to the racing community. It will be my job to heighten the profile of racing, both in the potential audience and to

The present Senior Steward Sir Thomas Pilkington.

Government. Racing is a major part of the leisure industry and in the next decade leisure will be the biggest industry in the country. The Jockey Club will have to strike a balance between being reactive and pro-active. I think we will be more active in certain areas, in an advisory role on things like training and marketing, and will be asking more questions to see how we can get a better product and press ahead to get a fairer price for that product. We've got to tell Government about what we provide for the country in employment and money, through tax and VAT. That way we will influence them. We don't want to make the mistake of calling it a subsidy. It is very definitely not a subsidy, it's a price for the product. Bookmakers are retailers and racing is the primary producer. We have been accused of being slow to move but I believe that quite often it is correct to move slowly. You want to be sure a perceived trend is an actual trend. Also we live in an age of consultation. The Stewards can't just sit down and say, "We'll do X, Y and Z".'

One of the immediate repercussions of Hartington's committee was the appointment of a salaried Chief Executive, from outside the Jockey Club's own ranks, to assist the incoming Senior Steward. On 10 August 1989, the Jockey Club announced that (from a short-list of four) Christopher Haines, a 50-year-old former major in the Rifle Brigade and latterly a high-powered technocrat in the sugar industry, would fill the position as of 2 October. Haines's racing experience could not, and did not, match his business expertise. He had acted as a Stipendiary Steward at low-key meetings during his army days in the Far East and had ridden in a few point-to-points. Hartington informed the media: 'Christopher Haines's input will be strategic and he will be advising us on ways and means forward. He will become a one-man HAC but will be working for the Jockey Club which, though it represents a great deal of the industry, does not have delegates from the industry.'

Haines's brief encompassed five main tasks:

1. To produce a strategic plan, including methods of implementation, for the Jockey Club, requiring him to focus on the Jockey Club's role within the racing industry over the next few years.
2. To be responsible for ensuring that the needs of the racing industry are effectively understood in Whitehall and Westminster.
3. To be responsible for the Jockey Club's financial planning, as agreed with the Administration and Finance Committee.
4. To be responsible for maintaining close liaison with the Levy Board, HAC and principal organisations represented there.
5. To report to and receive delegated authority from the Jockey Club Stewards.

Haines did not see himself as racing's new "supremo". 'I see my appointment as strengthening the existing tried-and-tested team, rather than replacing anyone. I don't see myself as some intellectual guru sitting in the office thinking up schemes. I hope anything I propose to the Stewards is entirely practical.' Haines began by refining the Club's management and operating structure. 'Coming from outside, one of my problems was having no historical knowledge of how the current situation had been arrived at. When a system builds up over such a long period of time things get blurred. In any organisation it's sensible to sit back, take a look and work out responsibilities. It was a fundamentally sound structure but it needed sharpening up and clarifying.'

Haines received a free hand. He confined himself to two basic objectives. Firstly, to recognise the different roles of the Stewards, their executive and Weatherbys; second, to simplify and clarify lines of communication. A Finance Steward replaced the Administration and Finance Committee; Jockey Club administration became the responsibility of the Deputy Chief Executive, a new post effectively replacing the Secretary to the Jockey Club –

though the traditional title of 'Keeper of the Match Book' was retained. Christopher Foster, the incumbent Secretary, was appointed; he would also look after rules and discipline. The Racecourse Steward assumed responsibility for security and integrity, which had previously resided with Administration and Finance, while forfeiting personnel to the Chief Executive, who thus had the right to "hire and fire". David Pipe was upgraded to Director of Public Affairs and made directly responsible to the Chief Executive – along with the directors of operations, development and planning and field services. The key move was seen to be the creation of a Finance Steward. 'Finance is a highly specialised and technical subject, far removed from racing horses, but it was being handled by committee,' explained Haines. 'The nature of our business is that we need to respond fast, with immediate technical input. By disbanding the committee and replacing it with a Steward with financial expertise and myself, we will get a direct, quicker and more responsive executive.' This vital job went to Christopher Spence.

The new broom sweeping Portman Square did not endear itself to every member of the Jockey Club, some of whom questioned the very need for a Chief Executive. 'If you've got any organisation with 100 to 119 members and one person is put into a position of power which hasn't existed before, it is not likely that 119 are going to say he is the most marvellous chap in the world,' reasons Sir Thomas Pilkington, who succeeded Lord Hartington as Senior Steward in 1994. 'And I think that would be the same in any company. The reaction was no different to what would have been expected whoever had been appointed.' The lukewarm reception was not lost on Haines himself: 'It's no secret that when I arrived there was no desk, no telephone, no secretary and not the greatest of welcomes. I was a Chief Executive with no executive. You couldn't have had a bigger mountain to climb and it took several months on a very hard and steep learning curve for me to understand and get to grips with the essential problems.'

Haines's critics were quick to harp on about his business background depriving him of the minutely detailed knowledge necessary to tackle racing's problems. Not as quotable as Hartington (or Pipe), Haines found himself dubbed "The Invisible Man" by the racing press who invariably wondered aloud on the nature of his role and what, if anything, he was actually achieving. Behind the scenes, however, Haines was beavering away – especially in the political arena. He acquired new advisers in GJW Consultants and engaged London Economics to provide a financial model for the industry. More importantly, he was exercising his talents as an accomplished lobbyist, honed during those days in the sugar industry, to fulfil his remit that the needs of racing were "more effectively understood at Westminster": David Pipe recalls the strategy: 'Lord Hartington had a lot of contact with MPs and politicians regarding racing's financial requirements. He and Christopher Haines realised very quickly that there was no way they could ever be met without a sympathetic parliamentary voice; and they set about improving Jockey Club relations with the Houses of Parliament. They ate and drank and dined and talked for racing practically every night of the week with politicians. I don't know how their constitutions stood it!'

While the public utterances of Christopher Haines may have cut little ice with journalists, those whispered behind closed doors proved far from ineffective. This romancing of Parliament generated a goodwill not entirely unconnected with the realisation of at least three prestigious targets, viz a reduction in general betting duty; valuable VAT concessions for owners; and the acceptance of Sunday racing.

Besides wooing Parliament, Lord Hartington was also conscious of the need to woo racing itself – or more specifically the many disparate factions which comprised the industry. Racing badly needed a united voice. In his first speech to the Gimcrack Club in December 1989 Hartington said: 'It is of immense concern to me when the public, and particularly their elected representatives, complain that racing does not seem to be able to make up its own mind on how it sees the future. How can an industry which is apparently divided in its own vision of the way ahead ever hope to gather sympathetic support in Westminster and Whitehall? Let us continue to represent our causes with vigour and imagination but let us also endeavour to display, on important matters of policy, a public unity which reflects the broad desire we all share to promote the best interests of racing.' In an effort to further this ambition Hartington convened an industry conference at Sandown Park on 23 April, 1990, inviting the chairmen of every body represented on the HAC and those who regularly attended the meetings – which thus added the bookmakers. 'At the end we will not issue an official communiqué, we will not compile an umpteen-point directive but we will all, every branch of the sport, be better informed of each others' expectations, fears, plans and suggestions and, crucially, it will help us identify the financial implications involved. Hopefully, understanding will generate consensus and racing can then prepare for the way ahead with a new and powerful unity.'

*Jockey Club Ring Inspector
monitoring betting at
Lingfield Park.*

"Shaping the Future", as the conference was called, generally met with widespread approval. Even Don Bruce had kind words for Hartington's initiative: 'As a bookmaker I go into conferences such as this with a degree of pessimism, thinking it's likely to be an exercise in which various parties will demand more money from us. But this one was very successful from our point of view because it was positive and more realistic. Individual sections can live in their own shells until somebody spells out the other side of the story, so the conference was worthwhile and the Jockey Club can be congratulated on having done it.' It was left to owner and breeder Bob McCreery (one of those who had resigned from HAC) to sound a warning note: 'Racing is brainwashed by the bookmaking lobby and that showed at the conference... one good thing that came out is that Lord Hartington, the Senior Steward, has got his ears open. Most of them in the past have had their ears and their eyes closed.'

Hartington was soon to give far clearer evidence of receptive – and perceptive – ears and eyes. From the meetings he and Haines had enjoyed with politicians and civil servants it was plain that unless racing could deliver an accountable and democratic body, Government would not pay heed to its entreaties, however much it may be inclined. The final push – the catalyst – proved to be the findings of Sir John Wheeler's all-party Home Affairs Select Committee inquiry into the industry's financial structure – the Levy and the Tote: there was no mention of the Jockey Club in the title of the investigation – which reported on 15 May, 1991. The message was crystal clear: 'It is vital in their own financial interests for the fragmented racing industry, through co-operation between the HAC and the Jockey Club, to find and follow strong and unified commercial leadership. Racing's power structure must be modernised to meet the challenge of the 1990s. To prosper, it must promote and sell itself on the domestic and international markets. It must become more efficient. It must look after its customers at every level. We believe that the racing industry will do itself a grave disservice if it does not unite behind a leadership with business acumen.'

The necessary reforms could not be achieved under the auspices of the Jockey Club: it could play a part but the Jockey Club alone was inadequate. The Club would be obliged to concede some of its traditional power base to a new body. Thus were the seeds of the British Horseracing Board firmly sewn.

Lord Hartington had to sell the idea to the Jockey Club members. He accomplished the task magnificently. Sir Thomas Pilkington remembers it well: 'The financial aspect, dependent on politics, had sunk home. Continuous journeys by the Jockey Club to the Houses of Parliament, which may have been done just as well by somebody else, were not going to achieve what a more broad-based body could achieve. It was becoming increasingly apparent we needed to achieve certain things with the help of Parliament and if the Jockey Club, however well it did everything, was going to be a barrier because of the self-electing oligarchy factor, then clearly that had to change. If it was going to change, it was better that it changed properly rather than cosmetically – that could have been done but it would not have worked. People outside the Jockey Club would be amazed at the enthusiasm with which members espoused the formation of the BHB. There was no campaign against it in general, only against a few specifics. This was undoubtedly due to Lord Hartington's powers of persuasion. It was most certainly a case of "Cometh the hour, cometh the man".'

Hartington unveiled his blueprint for racing in the 21st century during the course of his address at the Gimcrack Dinner in York on Tuesday, 17 December 1991 – some 24 hours after its approval by the Jockey Club's membership. 'In December 1977 the Jockey Club made public its submission to the Royal Commission on Gambling on the possible form of a future racing authority. *The Times* was sufficiently impressed to comment: "It is greatly to the credit of the Jockey Club that it has reassessed its former view and reached the conclusion it has now put forward. The reconsidered attitude can only be of benefit to racing." In the Committee's report the following year, Lord Rothschild accepted the Jockey Club's proposal for the establishment of a British Horseracing Authority. This, I must emphasise, was 14 years ago. In the event the Government could not accept the recommendation and the best alternative was found by the formation of the HAC. It is therefore worth remembering during these discussions on the structure of racing that not only have we been this way before, but also that it was the Jockey Club who pioneered the route. In July the Stewards appointed a study group to examine the

Racecourse enquiry.

Jockey Club Investigating Officer carrying out an inspection of trainer Henrietta Knight's schooling facilities.

options for change… the objective has been to produce a formula which would work, which had the potential both for improved commercial strength and for obtaining an increased return to racing from off-course betting, which had political and industry acceptability, and which could be introduced relatively quickly… consequently, the Stewards decided that any new board should be constructed in such a way that it, or its derivative, could potentially assume the functions of the Levy Board and the responsibility for the Tote at some point in the future. The proposal is that a British Horseracing Board be formed, which will be the body ultimately responsible for the direction of the racing industry. It will be responsible for strategic planning and policy, and would represent the industry in negotiation with the Government, whether on levy-related or other issues. It would be responsible for financial matters, fixtures and racecourse policy, public relations for the industry, promotion of the racing product and the industry's political aims… the Stewards believe that the proposal for a British Horseracing Board is the most practical step the Jockey Club can take to improve the position of the racing industry. At the moment the Jockey Club is held accountable for every aspect of racing, even though it may have no responsibility in that area. In future the situation will be very different. For racing as a whole, the buck will indeed stop at the British Horseracing Board. I believe the Jockey Club's view is clearly for change. I hope the industry will join us, and join us enthusiastically.'

The *Racing Post*'s "Revolution!" was not the only headline prompted by Hartington's disclosure. Others included: Jockey Club to loosen reins/Closing the book on an old thoroughbred/Jockey Club open door to a new era/Power shifting proposals are a step along the right road. Hartington's plan called for a board of ten members (later amended to 11) with four nominees from the Jockey Club (including Hartington as chairman), plus two each from the Racecourse Association, the Racehorse Owners Association and the HAC (subsequently known as the Industry Committee, it was eventually granted a third seat in recognition of the numerous interests – trainers, breeders, jockeys, stable staff, racegoers, transporters – HAC had represented). A structure working group was formed, chaired jointly by Lord Hartington and Sir Nevil Macready, chairman of HAC, and completed by John Cleverly, Peter Jones,

Stanley Jackson, Matthew McCloy, Sir Thomas Pilkington and Christopher Haines.

Ironically, after contributing so much to the BHB's formation, Christopher Haines was to be overlooked for the position of its first chief executive in favour of Tristram Ricketts, the chief executive of the Levy Board and, a double irony, the man Haines had pipped for the Jockey Club post in 1989. With the Jockey Club no longer requiring a chief executive in view of its refined workload, Christopher Haines found himself out of a job. It might, of course, have looked uncomfortably like the mixture as before if the Jockey Club's chief executive had been chosen. Haines held no grudge. 'I was not misled in any way by anybody at the Jockey Club about my job with them. But nobody had said to me when I took the job that they thought we had to make a new structure. The Home Affairs Select Committee concentrated the mind and expedited things.' However, he did admit to feeling a sense of pride emanating from his part in persuading the Jockey Club to accept the introduction of the BHB. 'It was never going to be easy to get it through but the arguments were rehearsed and played out over the months leading to creation and when the moment came it was absolutely clear that it was the strong will of the Club to proceed.' Christopher Haines will forever occupy a unique place in Jockey Club history: its first chief executive and its last; an architect of the BHB and thereby the architect of his own removal.

The embryo Board held informal talks in 1992, was formally established in January 1993 and assumed command on 10 June 1993. The inaugural Board comprised Lord Hartington (Chairman), Lord Zetland, David Oldrey and Christopher Spence from the Jockey Club; Sir Nevil Macready (Deputy Chairman; Industry), Lord Swaythling and Michael Darnell (Industry); Sir Paul Fox and John Sanderson (Racecourse Association); Nick Robinson and Peter Jones (Racehorse Owners Association). 'I believe the BHB is democratic, accountable and representative,' maintained the Chairman. 'We will provide a much needed focus for all those who want to see the sport they love progress to a state of sustained prosperity. This is the beginning. Today. It has got to work.'

Jockey Club judges Michael Hancock and Jonathan Dimsdale with the Hawkeye Camera which provides photofinish results in seconds.

Racing's new baby was subjected to microscopic scrutiny throughout its infancy. 'Let them have their honeymoon, they deserve it,' suggested Brough Scott, in his guise as Editorial Director of the *Racing Post*. 'Within two years of being told by the home Affairs Select Committee that racing had to put its administration into a new boat,

the good ship BHB was yesterday down the slipway and into open water. By any standards it was a real achievement… but the honeymoon will soon be over.' The Board instantly had to defend itself against the inevitable accusation of being nothing more than a redecorated Jockey Club. Speaking for one and all, Michael Darnell riposted: 'I will not support any movement to suggest this is the Jockey Club in a different guise'; Lord Hartington actually went so far as to put distance between the "new" and the "old": 'The Jockey Club will be accountable to us for the money they spend. We will expect value for money from the Jockey Club and I am confident they will deliver it.'

As the "honeymoon" drew to a close Hartington prepared himself for the flak which would surely follow. 'Having come from the Jockey Club, I am quite used to criticism and we are bound to make some mistakes,' he commented a touch wryly. By the time he stood down as Chairman in June 1996 (to be replaced by the former Tory cabinet minister, Lord Wakeham) media patience was running thin. The BHB's achievements were "mere minutiae" argued the army of Doubting Thomases. On the "big" issue – finance; a better deal from bookmakers, boosting prize money levels, acquisition of the Tote and Levy Board – progress had been "at least hesitant, at worst non-existent". In February 1996 the *Racing Post* ran a five-day series which analysed and appraised every facet of the BHB's work to date, incorporating the views of a panel of independent "experts" who marked each category out of ten. On the subject of racing's finances, for example, the Board received a total of 38 out of 90 for effort and a mere 29 out of 90 for achievement. In *Pacemaker*, Jocelyn de Moubray, in a piece headed "BHB is the Jockey Club in sheep's clothing" wrote scathingly: 'The continuities between the BHB's policies and those of the Jockey Club are far more obvious than any differences… the main difference between the BHB and the Jockey Club is that the BHB has real confidence and thus real power. The revolution in the administration of British racing is beginning to resemble the model repeated so many times in South America. The liberator wins a great victory over the forces of reaction; he resigns only to be reappointed by a grateful population who promptly lose all interest in the questions and problems which so stirred them and return to the preoccupations of their daily lives. Everything has to change so that nothing does.'

If Christopher Haines was the loser in the BHB power game "Stoker" (the nickname bestowed by his mother) Hartington was most definitely a winner. 'He was rightly hailed,' says David Pipe, 'as being the most outstanding administrator since Admiral Rous. He achieved an amazingly smooth transition.' Habitual critics of the Establishment readily concurred. Nick Robinson was suitably impressed by Hartington's performance at the BHB: 'Stoker's chairmanship has been excellent. He has invited anyone with anything to say to contribute on any subject. I never felt I'd been left out of a discussion even if he knew my views were contrary to the majority.' And Jocelyn de Moubray conceded: 'Since becoming Senior Steward, Hartington has succeeded in winning the confidence and support not only of racing's professionals and journalists but of Government as well, while for all practical purposes following the same policies.'

At the end of Hartington's term as Senior Steward the Jockey Club arguably found itself in better shape than ever before. Much of this was due to Hartington, who used the occasion of his farewell Gimcrack speech to stress the recent and ongoing contribution to racing from the Jockey Club. 'Let no one be under any illusion about the key role played by the Jockey Club in creating the BHB. Those who spoke disparagingly about "backwoodsmen clinging on to power" completely misread the situation. It was, in fact, the enthusiasm and vision displayed by members of the Jockey Club, coupled with a determination that this time the proposal should not founder, which ensured the successful formation of the BHB. I believe that the most important point about the creation of the Board is that it was done voluntarily by the Jockey Club and racing for racing. The Home Affairs Select Committee gave us a strong hint, which we took. Had that not been the case, sooner or later the Government would have taken the lead. I do not want racing to be run by any Government department, not now, not ever. He then drew attention to 'some of the crucially important work being done by the Jockey Club as part of our regulatory responsibilities: new ideas, new equipment, new techniques, new procedures, all directed toward improving facilities, management and cost effectiveness.' Flying physios and a new prototype skull cap were fresh initiatives to safeguard jockeys' welfare; security reviews and the development of an international programme to harmonise anti-doping policies were also in place.

The departing Senior Steward did, however, confess to certain frustrations: 'Initially, I was frustrated by the length of time it took to properly consult the industry. This has become much less frustrating because it has speeded up. Partly because a lot of people are still

Dr Michael Turner, the Jockey Club's Chief Medical Adviser, shows the greater protection offered by the new design of helmet (right).

doing the same thing and we have got to know each other a lot better across the industry. I sometimes do get frustrated by racing talking itself down. Racing has so many different attractions that it would be a pity for those to be forgotten.' And his outstanding achievement? 'The thing that I am most excited about is the fact that I do believe that racing's voice is now heard in Parliament, in Whitehall and I think that that is a result of the intention to create the BHB. It was an absolute precursor to the better relationship, better understanding and better communication with MPs and ministers. I think Christopher Haines deserves a great deal of credit as the architect of those two things.'

In July 1994 the Senior Steward's torch was passed to Thomas Henry Milborne-Swinnerton-Pilkington, 14th Baronet. Chairman of two shipping companies, the Charente Steamship Co. and the family firm of Thos & James Harrison Co and Deputy Chairman of Cluff Oil, Pilkington had latterly been Chairman of Newmarket Racecourses Trust in addition to chairing the Jockey Club's Race Planning Committee and serving on the Levy Board.

Pilkington's Jockey Club defined its four main objectives as:

1. To regulate horseracing in Great Britain to the highest standards.
2. Through nominees to BHB, to support the Board's work in administering the best interests of horseracing and developing the sport, including breeding.
3. To operate racecourses to high technical and commercial standards for the benefit of racing generally.
4. To operate first class training facilities.

Objectives 3 and 4 centred on Racecourse Holdings Trust (its group of racecourses increased to 12 with the acquisition of Epsom, Sandown and Kempton in 1994) and the Jockey Club Estates, which administers the Newmarket Training Grounds, various local properties and the Jockey Club Rooms. After the formation of the BHB the Stewards felt it essential to emphasise the Jockey Club as a "family" of activities with a common interest. Consequently, both racecourses and training grounds were expected to function as centres of excellence in their respective fields. For instance, declining attendance figures – and, to be frank, the declining kudos – of the Derby was a source of concern to the incoming Senior Steward. 'It has slipped rather disastrously. One thing that has to be done is the total resuscitation of that meeting and the restoring of the Derby to pre-eminence. The Grand National has now come right back to what it used to be and so must the Derby. Apart from the Derby, the Oaks and the Coronation Cup, the racing at the meeting is not up to much and something has to be done to bring the crowds back. Perhaps a change of day.' Action was swift. The 1995 Derby was run on a Saturday and resulted in a paid attendance 3% up on 1994. The trend continued in 1996 and 1997 and the 1998 Derby will also be run on a Saturday. Only a small step but one in the right direction. As Pilkington freely admits: 'A lot of work needs to be put in.'

The two fundamental responsibilities awaiting the new Senior Steward were to ensure that a cordial working relationship existed with the BHB and to oversee the rigorous application of the Club's mandate as racing's regulatory body. 'The Jockey Club and the BHB are working well in tandem. We're very involved as partners and there's no feeling of being overlooked or overshadowed. Our input to the BHB through our four members is viewed as one of the cornerstones for the Jockey Club of the future. We don't, of course, have a majority now. But we will be contributing and we are going to have a major influence.'

The removal of the Jockey Club's direct obligations on the financial front acted as a distinct spur to its traditional obligations re matters of security, discipline and integrity. David Pipe explains: 'The regulator is open all the time to criticism from people within racing who don't agree with some decisions taken on the racecourse – for whatever reason – and there tends to be a great furore for a time. These thoroughly unpopular perceptions of the regulator tend to move across to all the other things you're doing, in race planning or finance, for example. The new division of responsibility is, therefore, quite useful to the BHB, since they aren't now tarred with that particular brush. With the setting-up of the BHB, the Jockey Club has been able to lay more emphasis on the regulatory issue, which it was originally formed to do. There hasn't subsequently been any special "crackdown" but we've taken a rather stronger line.'

The Jockey Club's new-found vigour found expression in a wide-ranging review of its disciplinary function by a five-man committee chaired by Anthony Mildmay-White, who had assumed chairmanship of the Disciplinary Committee in January 1993. The group's report appeared in February 1994. Mildmay-White stressed the immediate priority was to produce a new Disciplinary Committee and management structure which would (1) continue to provide a tribunal system which was seen to be fair; (2) raise the standard

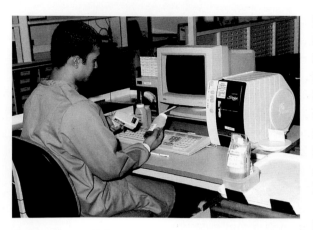

A dope testing sample has its bar-code checked in on arrival at the Horseracing Forensic Laboratory.

in the selection, training and assessment of Local Stewards; (3) improve assistance to those Local Stewards in carrying out their duties; (4) organise educational programmes for Local Stewards, Stewards' Secretaries, Jockeys and the Press; (5) reinforce and improve the Monitoring System; (6) provide an appropriate staff at Portman Square to ensure a proactive and credible approach to the full range of Disciplinary Procedures.

In order to fulfil these commitments three important changes to the Club's management structure were recommended viz (1) a reconstituted Disciplinary Committee; (2) a new senior management post; (3) a redefined middle management post. By 1996 the necessary measures had been taken. In September 1994 Malcolm Wallace, previously Director General of the British Equestrian Federation, became Director of Regulation, covering both discipline and licensing. The permanent link at Portman Square for the 290 Local Stewards, Wallace was made responsible for overseeing their training and that of the 13 Stewards' Secretaries, the "stipes". At the same time a new position was created, Analyst for the Monitoring System, whose brief was to check the quality and consistency of decisons made by local Stewards through the rigorous scrutiny of race videos, thereby building up an extensive library to illustrate any breaches of the Rules that could be used for educational and training purposes.

The heavier work-load that would inevitably result from these improvements necessitated an increase in the size of the Disciplinary Committee, which was enlarged by five members and split in two – a Judicial arm and a Stewarding arm. The former comprised those members who sat on enquiries at Portman Square; the five new members made up the Stewarding arm and, effectively, constituted the Disciplinary Committee on the racecourse – each being directly responsible for 12 racecourses. The improved contact between the Disciplinary Committee and Local Stewards yielded more effective two-way flow of information and a greater insight into the performance of individual panels.

The establishment of this new structure depended for its success upon a consistent level of performance from local Stewards. To that end – rather than introduce a system of professional Stewards – considerable thought was put into producing a revamped programme of education, in particular the training of chairmen. The new Trainee Stewards Scheme involved (1) a day spent with each of the different officials who act on the racecourse, at a variety of tracks; approximately ten days in all; (2) a New Stewards Seminar, which included a written examination. After this initial period of training those approved became "probationary" Stewards. Under the old system, by contrast, new Stewards were appointed to a panel on a probationary basis after just two days of training. In addition, a two-day new Chairmen's Seminar would be held annually, encompassing a written examination, a video questionnaire on selected racecourse incidents and a practical assessment of ability in chairing a panel of Stewards at an enquiry. This augmented the five Chairmen's Seminars already held annually in different parts of the country; the 13 Stewards Secretaries were kept abreast of Disciplinary Committee policy via a series of training days throughout the year.

Consistent and efficient stewarding was essential in view of fundamental changes to the Rules governing the use of the whip and treatment for cases of interference. The vexed question of the whip – or, to be more precise, misuse of the whip – had hovered over racing ever since the public outcry following an unsavoury exhibition of whip-wielding by two Irish jockeys during the Cheltenham National Hunt Festival of 1980. In the face of increasing infringements tough new restrictions were introduced which culminated in March 1988 with the recommendation that 'Stewards should consider enquiring into any case where a rider has used his whip more than 10 times, either in a Flat race or after the penultimate obstacle in a steeplechase or hurdles race.' More significantly, punishments kept pace with the crimes; bans replaced fines. With every tightening of Instruction H9 the number of causes celebres multiplied. Things came to a head in 1992 when three-times champion Steve Cauthen – hardly anyone's idea of a whip-happy jockey – was referred to Portman Square for twice hitting mounts down the shoulder. Cauthen chose to make a stand on behalf of his beleaguered colleagues. A subsequent high-profile appeal during which Cauthen implored the Jockey Club to rethink its attitude to the use of the whip seemed to have failed miserably as Cauthen wound up with a 10-day ban. The Disciplinary Committee, however, did subsequently take a fresh look at H9. To the jockeys' chagrin, a working party (two trainers, two vets, two jockeys) led by Sir Piers Bengough suggested that the threshold for "hits" should be halved to just five and, moreover, use of the whip should be restricted to shoulder height. The new threshold, it was emphasised, remained only a "trigger mechanism" designed to encourage Stewards to examine the riding of that jockey.

The application of Rule 153 which dealt with interference had long been a thorn in the Jockey Club's side as regards provoking the kind of "great furore" of which David Pipe spoke. In January 1994 the Jockey Club, for the first time, accepted the principle of separating the treatment of horse and rider, albeit only in the category of "careless" riding. As of April 1994 any horse winning a race on merit but whose rider had committed a minor infringement would keep the race, although the jockey would be deemed guilty of an offence: previously, a horse causing interference due to its jockey's careless riding had to be relegated even if the result was clearly unaffected.

In company with these two fundamental areas of change came a new system of penalties for riding offences. Automatic referral to Portman Square after the third offence of the season was scrapped: in its stead came a tottingup procedure whereby jockeys suspended for 12 or more days for either inter-ference or misuse of the whip – but not a combination of the two since statis-tics suggested jockeys who offend under one category rarely did so under the other – were to be referred to the Disciplinary Committee on the next occa-sion they committed the same offence. Any rider found in breach received a minimum of 14 days suspension on top of the appropriate suspension for the said offence; all jockeys started with a clean sheet every 1st January.

At the other end of the spectrum, uppermost in the mind of the Jockey Club's chief medical adviser, Dr Michael Turner, as the 1990s reached the half-way point, was the fitness, diet and general wellbeing of jockeys. He sought to raise jockeys' awareness, particularly regarding some of the harmful ways they chose to control their weight. A further sign of the times was the introduction of random tests for drugs – though the line was drawn at the waggish suggestion of a similar test for alcohol being initiated for Stewards!

The Jockey Club continued its war against the doping of racehorses. Despite ever improving security measures in the wake of two proven cases of doping in 1990 (both Bravefoot and Norwich were "got-at" with a quick-act-ing tranquilliser in the racecourse stables an hour before running at Doncaster) the possibility of dope being administered to a racehorse can never be eliminated entirely. But, in the world of modern forensic science, there is only one way the drug can escape detection and that is if the horse escapes detection in running and is not dope-tested. 'Doping a horse is not difficult,' says Neville Dunnett, Director of the Horseracing Forensic Laboratory which annually tests some 7,500 samples on behalf of the Jockey Club, 'but doping a horse so that we cannot detect it is very, very difficult indeed. We are as con-fident as can be that we can identify any drug that will affect a horse's perfor-mance.' The European Horserace Scientific Liaison Committee, established by the Racing authorities of Britain, Ireland and France to co-ordinate approaches to anti-doping control and continuing research into emerging problems in the illicit use of drugs, had held its first meeting in July 1992.

Originally, the one fish which seemed to have eluded the Jockey Club's capacious disciplinary net was the "non-trier". 'Racing is a sport prone to skulduggery and calculated breaches of the Rules but all the evidence I have suggests that the incidence of non-triers is nowhere near as great as people believe,' said Mildmay-White in 1994. 'We do look at all those horses that have had comments such as "given as easy time" and in 98% of cases there is a valid reason or the case is not actionable under Rule 151, which is one of the more difficult Rules to make a charge stick. I don't believe there is any-thing wrong with the Rule or with the instructions to Stewards about how to spot non-triers but because of public concern it may be an area we need to monitor more closely. We must certainly never be over-confident.' The prob-lem was soon addressed by a package of stringent measures that took effect in March 1995. In cases where jockey and trainer were found to have prevented a horse from running on its merits, to deceive the handicapper or set up a betting coup, the horse would be banned from running for up to 30 days; fines continued to be the punishment meted out to trainers but suspensions, once again, constituted the preferred medicine for jockeys – up to 14 days for repeated offence. Additional impetus to this campaign materialised in 1996 when it became mandatory for trainers to make public any reasons that emerged for a poor performance before the said animal ran again – or face a fine. 'We are shutting the door on the trainer who comes before an enquiry into a horse's improvement in form and says, "Well, he had sore shins last time".'

Jockey Club Veterinary Officer checks the heart rate of a horse selected to provide a post-race sample.

In a little over three years as Chairman of the Disciplinary Committee, Anthony Mildmay-White, had masterminded arguably the greatest ever shake-up in Jockey Club disciplinary procedure. As one might expect, neither jockeys nor trainers exactly greeted his blitzkrieg with unfettered glee. 'One of the aims that the review of the disciplinary function had, was that those involved in decisons taken by Local Stewards and the Jockey Club, and the general public, should have confidence in the system. Everything that we are doing is trying to achieve that. Ultimately, we're here for the integrity and safety of racing. And, therefore, we have to take decisions which are sometimes unpalatable. But that is something the Disciplinary Committee can live with.'

The same could be said of the Jockey Club *per se* as, with the imminent arrival of the next Millennium, it tackles its role as racing's guardian with renewed gusto. 'Guardianship sounds slightly pompous,' admits Sir Thomas Pilkington, 'but standards arc important in everything that the Jockey Club does. If racing is to flourish – and we want racing in Britain to be at the top; the best in the world in all ways – these standards must of necessity be high and our effort to maintain them must be rigorous.

"The Jockey Club is now able to concentrate on its clearly defined role as racing's regulatory body. The standards are being set and maintained."

Acknowledgements

The author would like to thank all the staff of the Jockey Club and the British Horseracing Board for their kind assistance with this book, and in particular the following:

Lt Col. Brian Abraham
Peter Amos
Col. Sir Piers Bengough
Roger Buffam
Fiona Campion
Christopher Foster
Geoffrey Gibbs
Frank Griffin
Christopher Haines
Marquess of Hartington
David Hillyard
The late John Hislop
Nigel Macfarlane
Anthony Mildmay-White
Sir Thomas Pilkington
David Pipe
Richard Smith
Dr. Michael Turner
Marquess of Zetland

With special thanks to Caroline Buttle, Club Administrator, and Franca Holden for decyphering the original typescript. He would also like to thank Gerry Cranham for his photographs on pages 63, 85, 125, 126, 154, 157, 166, the Mary Evans Picture Library for those on pages i and 32, and the Jockey Club for other recent pictures.

Bibliography

A Social and Economic History of Horse Racing – Wray Vamplew
Bailey's Magazine
Cromwell, Chief of Men – Antonia Fraser
English Social History – G.M. Trevelyan
Fred Archer – His Life and Times – John Welcome
Genius Genuine – Samuel Chifney, Snr
History of the British Turf – James Christine Whyte
Horse Power – The Politics of the Turf – Christopher R. Hill
Horse in Training
Jockey Club Archives, Reports etc.
Kings of the Turf – 'Thormanby'
Men and Horses I Have Known – Hon. George Lambton
My Story – Gordon Richards
Northern Turf History – J. Fairfax-Blakeborough
Oxford Encyclopaedia
Raceform
Ruff's Guide to the Turf
Tattersalls' Archives
The Biographical Encyclopaedia of British Flat Racing – P. Willett
The Encyclopaedia of Flat Racing – Howard Wright
The Encyclopaedia of Steeplechasing – Patricia Smyly
The *Guardian*
The Heath and the Turf – R. Onslow
The History of Steeplechasing – M. Seth-Smith, P. Willett, R. Mortimer, J. Lawrence
The Jockey Club and its Founders – R. Black
The Jockey Club – R. Mortimer
The Laws and the Practice of Horse Racing – Hon. Admiral H.J. Rous
The Knavesmire Story – John Stevens
The Paddock Book – Robert Rodrigo
The Racing Calendar
The *Racing Post*
The *Sporting Life*
The *Sunday Chronicle*
The Times
The Turf of Old – Denzil Batchelor
The Winter Kings – Ivor Herbert and Patricia Smyly
The Yellow Earl – Douglas Sutherland
They're Off! – Anne Alcock
Timeform
Tod Sloan by Himself – Tod Sloan
Turf Annals – John Orton
Weatherbys

Index

References in *italics* are to pages with illustrations only.